A Divine Healing Journey

A Divine Healing Journey

Let Jesus Be Your Guide

Tina Hightower Garrett
Wandah Mitchell Parenti

Copyright © 2022 by Tina Hightower Garrett and
Wanda Mitchell Parenti

All rights reserved. In accordance with the U.S. Copyright Act of 1976, the scanning, uploading, and electronic sharing of any part of this book without the permission of the publisher constitute unlawful piracy and theft of the author's intellectual property. Reviewers may quote brief passages in reviews. If you would like to use material from the book (other than for review purposes), prior written permission must be obtained by contacting the publisher at:

books@walton publishinghouse.com
Walton Publishing House
Houston, Texas
www.waltonpublishinghouse.com
Printed in the United States of America

The advice found within may not be suitable for every individual. This work is purchased with the understanding that neither the author nor the publisher is held responsible for any results. Neither author nor publisher assumes responsibility for errors, omissions, or contrary interpretations of the subject matter herein. Any perceived disparagement of an individual or organization is a misinterpretation.

Brand and product names mentioned are trademarks that belong solely to their respective owners. POWER Moms© book and products are owned by H.E. Dr. Sherrie Walton and used with permission. Library of Congress Cataloging-in-Publication Data under

ISBN: 978-1-953993-38-0 (Hardback)
ISBN: 978-1-953993-37-3 (Paperback)
ISBN: 978-1-953993-39-7 (Ebook/Digital)

Table of Contents

Family Ties 15
- Week 1: Why is Revelation Necessary? 17
- Week 2: Is Your Secret Safe? 20
- Week 3: The Great Heart Surgeon 23
- Week 4: Don't Stop Dreaming 27

Life Interrupted 31
- Week 5: Use It or Lose It 33
- Week 6: Miracles Usually Don't Happen the
  Way We Imagine 36
- Week 7: The Wrestling Match has already Been Won 40
- Week 8: Travel Light 43

Behind the Veil 47
- Week 9: Don't Lose Your Peace 49
- Week 10: What is Your Identity? 52
- Week 11: Look in the Mirror 54
- Week 12: Becoming 57

Worthy 61
- Week 13: What Are We Thinking About? 63
- Week 14: Who is Your Teacher? 66
- Week 15: Breathe 69
- Week 16: I Am Enough 72

Seasons of Drought 75
- Week 17: Infertility 77
- Week 18: He is in the Middle 79
- Week 19: Obey When it Doesn't Make Sense 82
- Week 20: Wait 85

Panicked and Paralyzed 89
- Week 21: How Are You Prioritizing Your Time? 91
- Week 22: Angels Are Watching Over Us! 94
- Week 23: Tell the Mountain to Move 97
- Week 24: Slow Down 100

Battlefield of the Mind 103
- Week 25: Battlefield of the Mind 105
- Week 26: Training for Battle 108
- Week 27: Are You Facing Your Giant? 111
- Week 28: Undefeated 114

No More Shackles 117
- Week 29: Let's Keep the Grave Clothes Off 119
- Week 30: Let's Change our Perspective 121
- Week 31: Early in the Morning 124
- Week 32: One Touch 126

Our Daily Prayer 129
- Week 33: The Lord's Prayer 131
- Week 34: Are you Hoping for Something that Hasn't Happened Yet? 133
- Week 35: Reminders 136
- Week 36: Speak Intentionally 139

An Heir 141
- Week 37: What Is Your Legacy? 143
- Week 38: We Are Uniquely Made 146
- Week 39: Are You an Upright Person? 149
- Week 40: What Proof Do You Need? 152

Keep it Pushing 155
- Week 41: Who is Your Firefighter? 157
- Week 42: Shout a Little Louder 160
- Week 43: Favor is Not Fair 163
- Week 44: Stay Charged Up 166

All is Not Lost 169
- Week 45: It's Not a Secret! 171
- Week 46: We are Anchored 174
- Week 47: You Are Stronger Than You Think 177
- Week 48: Restoration 180

An Attitude of Gratitude 183
- Week 49: Our Attitude Determines our Gratitude 185
- Week 50: Small Things Still Matter 189
- Week 51: There is a Plan for "Your" Purpose 192
- Week 52: What is Your Story? 195

Hello Overcomers!

One of my favorite ways to start off my day is by reading a devotional while sipping a good cup of coffee or tea. For me, it's a combination of studying the Bible and hearing a wonderful message. Here's how I started writing devotionals.

I belong to a Women's Ministry group called Grace Living Ministries. When the pandemic took everyone by surprise, the founder and spiritual leader, Regina Leachman, started a weekly Bible Study group on Zoom to keep women spiritually connected. An individual in our study group voluntarily started texting us devotionals every day. I was ecstatic! Devotionals arriving by text every morning at 6 a.m., what a welcomed and much-needed surprise!

One day our Bible study leader asked me if I would like to share in writing the devotionals every week. I said sure, but in my mind, I was thinking where do I start? Keep in mind I love to read devotions, but I do not write them. It's like being a movie enthusiast and someone says, "Would you like to direct a movie?" Led by faith, I started writing devotionals and was filled with joy.

Now, along with myself, devotionals are collectively being written by several people every week. These devotionals are circulated to individuals, various groups and churches. My relationship with God went to a different height and I found a hidden passion that I didn't realize existed. I started seeing Him differently. God started speaking to me in ways I never imagined. His words were revealed to me in small yet significant ways; like watching a bird in the tree chirping, flowers blooming in the spring or summer, and the cerulean blue sky. We serve a God that reaches out to us in so many ways. When I'm writing devotionals, God gives me a vision of writing illustrative stories that connect yesterday with today. Jesus spoke in parables. In the book of Ecclesiastes,

Solomon, the man of wisdom said, "there's nothing new under the sun."

When reading the devotionals from *A Divine Healing Journey*, my heart's desire is for you to forge a closer relationship with the Creator. These devotionals speak about depression, anxiety, success, and failures. Most importantly each devotional was written from my heart to give everyone a sense of hope in Christ Jesus. God's word heals the soul. I also want to use these devotionals to encourage everyone regardless of where they are in their spiritual journey, to take their personal relationship with God to a higher level. We can't wait to take this 52-week journey with you. Whether you've never read the Bible before or are a Bible Scholar, our prayer is that you will finish this journey with a different perspective on why you were created and find healing in the areas of mental, spiritual, emotional, and relational growth on this divine healing journey. All aboard, the journey is about to begin!

Blessings and favor,

Tina

When I was a very young girl, my 6th grade teacher, Mrs. Kirby introduced me to writing. She would bring pictures to class, depicting a red balloon flying up in the sky, the perfect vanilla ice cream cone, or a lone empty telephone booth. She'd ask us to look at the picture, and write about what we saw, and how the picture made us feel. It was there I developed a love for writing. I could express myself creatively. I could dream, and share my thoughts, and feelings. So, I began writing short stories, poems, and songs, which also inspired me to keep a journal, not a diary, but a journal. Don't get me wrong. I am not opposed to diaries at all. But my journaling allowed me to talk more in-depth about my feelings, hopes, dreams, and desires. My journal was where my relationship with God really started to grow. Starting, or ending each day with a letter to my Heavenly Father was the best part of each day. I looked forward to it every day. Establishing and nurturing a relationship with someone requires that you spend time with them. How close you two become, and how strong that relationship becomes, will depend on how often you spend time nurturing it. The relationship that I have now with Christ, is largely due to what started years ago in my journal. Now understand, that's my story. It's never too late to start spending time with your Heavenly Father, or to build a close, loving relationship with Him. You can literally start today. Some people will say to just spend time in His Word. That is great. We should certainly read His Word, but for some that can also be quite overwhelming, and frankly, challenging. Taking it one day at a time, reading a few scriptures at a time daily, reading words of affirmation to encourage, and empower you daily, baby steps can lead you to the most amazing relationship with your Heavenly Father.

With *A Divine Healing Journey* devotional and journal, you can write Him a love letter, short message, or a note. He knows exactly what's in your heart. In fact, He knows what you will say before you say it. He also knows those things you don't say. The important part is that you are spending time with Him, building, and nurturing your relationship with Him. That's what He created us for, relationship. The Word of God says in Revelation 3:20, "Behold, I stand at the door and knock. If anyone who hears my voice, and opens the door, I will come into him and eat with him, and he with me." Writing in my journal daily and abiding with Him has literally changed my life. I encourage you to journey with us, open this book daily and allow God to come in and eat with you.

Peace, Love and Blessings,

Wandah

Devotionals

Family Ties

WEEK #1

Why is Revelation Necessary?

Psalm 19:1-2 (ESV)

"The heavens declare the glory of God, and the sky above proclaims his handiwork. Day to day pours out speech, and night to night reveals knowledge."

Without revelation, we wouldn't know who God is. Our loving Heavenly Father still reveals the truth to us. Revelation comes in various ways: a still, small voice; profound spiritual promptings; visions, and others.

What has God revealed to you this year? As I reflected on my vision board, God revealed to me that almost everything came to life. I was amazed!

Let's be mindful of what God is revealing to us. He reveals his message to us in small things as well as large things. The Word reveals His plans and purpose for our lives. "If any of you lack wisdom, you should ask God, who gives generously to all without finding fault, and it will be given to you. James 1:5. (NIV)

God revealed himself to Hagar, an Egyptian slave while she was in the wilderness by saying "I see you." Genesis 16:12 (NIV) God delivered her and her son Ishmael from the desert. There are times in our lives when we feel as though we are alone. Be confident that you are not alone. We are sometimes found in a place of desperation and loneliness. God was with

Hagar and her son. An angel of The Lord appeared to her when she was on her last leg. She received a promise from God that she and her son would be okay. Perhaps our story isn't the same as Hagar's, however we can relate to God rescuing us. The same God that came to Hagar's aid is the same God that will continue to come to our aid.

Prayer

> **Lord, I know that You will reveal all the plans designed for my life. The revelation that I cling to is to always feel your presence. I want to see Your reverence in my daily life through the sounds of birds, the rain, babies crying and people laughing. Thank you for revealing how much You love me. In Jesus' name, Amen!**

Reflection

> Revelation comes in various ways: a still, small voice; profound spiritual promptings; visions, and others.

WEEK #2

Is Your Secret Safe?

Judges 16:6 (NIV)

So Delilah said to Samson, "Tell me the secret of your great strength and how you can be tied up and subdued."

Have you ever shared something confidential with someone and they told someone else? Or, has someone told you a secret and you shared it with someone else? Maybe you felt pressured to say something because you were being questioned. This is how Samson felt.

Then she said to him, "How can you say, 'I love you,' when you won't confide in me? This is the third time you have made a fool of me and haven't told me the secret of your great strength." Judges 16:15-17 (NIV)

With such nagging, she prodded him day after day until he was sick to death of it. So, he told her everything. "No razor has ever been used on my head," he said, "because I have been a Nazirite dedicated to God from my mother's womb. If my head were shaved, my strength would leave me, and I would become as weak as any other man."

Delilah nagged Samson until he broke down and told her that his strength would be lost if his head were shaved. She was relentless! Delilah then told the Philistines and had someone come and shave Samson's head. This robbed him of his powers. In this way, Samson lost his powers by giving away his secret to someone who was only pretending to love him. Beware when someone says, "Your secret is safe with me." This is how Delilah tricked Samson.

Sometimes people will conspire together to seek information that will benefit them. Delilah was sold out for eleven hundred pieces of silver. Judges 16:4 (NIV)

Samson told Delilah a secret that cost him his life. There's nothing wrong with sharing information about ourselves to a trusted source. There are times when we need to talk to someone about what we're experiencing. However, we should remember that Jesus is available 24/7 and our secrets are always safe with Him!

Prayer

> **Dear God, let us honor You by not sharing information that someone has trusted us with. Lord let us stay mindful about committing to secrecy. When people confide in us, let them feel confident that we will bring their cares to only You and not to anyone else. Control our thoughts and actions so that they line up with Your word. In Jesus' name, Amen!**

> Beware when someone says, "Your secret is safe with me." This is how Delilah tricked Samson.

WEEK #3

The Great Heart Surgeon

John 14:27 (NIV)

"Peace I leave with you; my peace I give you. I do not give to you as the world gives. Do not let your hearts be troubled and do not be afraid."

As we're traveling through this world, on our journey to where God is taking us, we will experience heartbreaks along the way by someone whom we trusted. Do you remember your first heartbreak? Was it caused by a parent, boyfriend, or a girlfriend? What was your heartbreak?

Do we break Jesus' heart when we disobey Him? The Bible indicates that Jesus felt emotions.

Can you imagine how Jesus must have felt when Adam and Eve disobeyed Him? How about when Judas and Peter betrayed him? One more, He asked Moses to strike the rock and he hit it in anger!

John 11:35 (KJV) says "Jesus wept." How do we turn heartbreaks into happiness? We let God perform open heart surgery on our hearts. The word of God is the best scalpel!

Hebrews 4:12 (KJV) says "For the word of God is quick, and powerful, and sharper than any two-edged sword, piercing even to the dividing asunder of soul and spirit, and of the joints and marrow, and is a discerner of the thoughts and intents of the heart."

Our hearts play a very vital role in our spiritual, mental and health condition. We need our heart to function, and we also need our heart to serve God. He does a wonderful job on repairing hearts. That's why he's known as The Great Physician. His blood runs through our veins like a river flowing into the ocean.

Here are a few verses that can help us when we're feeling broken hearted:

"First we have to believe that God loves us and has worked everything out for our good." Romans 8:28 (NIV)

We must "trust in the Lord without all our hearts and lean not on our own understanding." Proverbs 3:5-6 (NIV)

Usually after a heartbreak we come to the conclusion that it worked out for our good. I know firsthand because I've experienced this. I married my high school sweetheart and was heartbroken when the marriage ended. I later learned that it was the best thing that could have happened for me. The key is to not let your heartbreak break your heart.

God communicates with us through this most important organ, our hearts. David truly understood this when he said, "Create in me a pure heart, O God, and renew a steadfast spirit within me." Psalm 51:10 (NIV)

He also "heals the brokenhearted and binds up their wounds." Psalm 147:3 (NIV)

As children and adults, we are not responsible for our hearts being broken; we are responsible for taking our hearts to Jesus for open heart surgery. By His stripes we are healed!

Prayer

> Lord, I come to You asking that You protect my heart and keep it clean so that I can worship You, love You, obey You and exalt your Holy name. In Jesus' name I pray, Amen!

Reflection

Our hearts play a very vital role in our spiritual, mental and health condition.

WEEK #4

Don't Stop Dreaming

Isaiah 55:8 (NKJV)

"For My thoughts are not your thoughts, Nor are your ways My ways," says the Lord.

Has God given you a dream or a vision that you haven't fulfilled yet? As a child I had an imagination that was out of this world. In fact, I still do. As an adult, I have come to realize that my imagination is really a dream, a vision or hope. Am I disappointed when things don't turn out the way I expected? Of course! Sometimes our dreams are right in front of us, however, they look different from what we imagined.

Children are not afraid of dreaming, primarily, because they are innocent. Even during a difficult childhood, children have the ability to escape their current situation in hopes of a better tomorrow. Some of us have experienced hurt, loss, grief, and pain. Because of this, we have stopped dreaming. Well, today is a new day! Through our pain God still gives us dreams and visions. It's called hope and faith. Joseph, Solomon, Jacob, Samuel, Paul, and others are examples of having dreams inspired by God.

Here is a story about a famous king, King David, who also had a dream, but his dream was shattered. We read the story in 2 Samuel 7 and 1 Chronicles 17. King David dreamed of building a temple for God. Unlike Jabez, who only told his dream to God, King David told his dream to the Prophet Nathan. As Nathan listened, he responded, just like we might: "Go for it!" But in the middle of the night, God spoke to the prophet and told him to go and tell David emphatically *No! I do not want you to build me a temple!* Sheepishly Nathan takes what God said and returns to David with His message. There was nothing wrong with David's dream. He wanted, just like Jabez, to honor God but the Heavenly Father had something even better in store for David!

After Nathan told David what God said, David had a choice. When we hear God say "no" we also have choices. We can say, *God, you are being unfair,* or *you and others are against me*. We can choose to be bitter, angry, or have a temper tantrum or submit. So, what did David do when his dream was shattered? He went and sat before the Lord.

You may have a dream and it seems as if God is not listening. Like Jabez and King David, your heart is pure. You just want to honor and glorify God, but He has said "no." God didn't take away King David's dream but showed David that His dream was far better and bigger than even David could think or imagine. Don't stop listening when the Lord says no. Why? He usually has something far greater or bigger than you can ever imagine. God is listening! God cares but we may have missed his bigger dream because we are too busy whining. Sit before God and listen to His still, small voice.

Let's work on putting aside all of those things that are prohibiting us from achieving our dreams that God has for us. The Word says, "People perish because of a lack of vision." Proverbs 29:18 Have the faith that your dreams have already been answered. Pursuing our dreams will not only make a difference in our lives, but it will also have an impact on others as well!

Prayer

> Lord, let my dreams and desires line up with Your plans for my life. I come to You without reservations. I put my trust in You. Let me listen to Your calm and loving voice that will draw me nearer and nearer to You. Thank You, Jesus!

Reflection

Through our pain God still gives us dreams and visions. It's called hope and faith.

Let's work on putting aside all of those things that are prohibiting us from achieving our dreams that God has for us.

WEEK #5

Use It or Lose It

The Parable of the Talents teaches that God always gives us everything we need to do for what he has called us to do. This was the case of the men with the talents. The last man with the least amount of talent hid what God had given him. The Bible states that God was angry. He took from the man with one talent and gave it to the man with the most. Why? Because the man with the most trusted God and invested what was given to him.

Are we investing what God has given us? Our time, our gifts, our testimonies? How can we grow if we're not using what He has given us? Are we waiting for the right time and missing out on what's in front of us? The Lord doesn't plant desires in our hearts without a purpose. God is intentional; therefore, we must be intentional. God has given each one of us a specific talent that must be used or we will lose it. If we don't, He will give it to someone else.

Have you ever had an idea about inventing something and someone beat you to it? Is there something that has been tugging at your heart, but you keep putting it off? Doing so can cause us to miss that *Kairos* moment that can expire if we don't act upon it. Kairos (Ancient Greek: καιρός) is an Ancient Greek word meaning "the right, critical, or opportune moment."

What happens to fruit when it's not picked at the appropriate time? It rots. We must plant another seed, wait, and start over. It's the same as missing that Kairos moment. Oftentimes, we are convinced that it's not the right time either through fear or doubt. However, if God places a desire in our hearts, it's vital that we act on it and not wait for a time when we feel comfortable. In my life, the unbelievable blessings appeared when I felt uncomfortable because I fully relied on God.

The children of Israel waited and when they were ready to cross over, Moses indicated that it was too late. The Lord had retracted the commandment to go up and possess the land, and, therefore, if they went up then, they would go without His power (Numbers 14:40-45) We can't do anything without God's power. They eventually crossed over and defeated the Canaanites because they didn't seize the opportunity. Has this ever happened to you? When we do something without God's power it's because we didn't move when He said to move. The children of Israel did defeat the Canaanites, but they had to wait, so it was a delayed victory. Use what God has given you. Don't miss your Kairos moment!

Prayer

> **Lord, let me recognize the talents and gifts that You have planted inside of me. I don't want to overlook these gifts. Give me the courage and motivation to pursue what You've given me. Place me in the company of people that will water these gifts! In Jesus' name, Amen!**

Reflection

God has given each one of us a specific talent that must be used or we will lose it.

WEEK #6

Miracles Usually Don't Happen the Way We Imagine

Naaman had a lot going for him. He was captain of the army of the King of Syria. However, what he had against him was devastating; he was a leper, which meant that he had a horrible, incurable disease that would slowly result in his death. No matter how good and successful everything else was in Naaman's life, he was a leper.

A young girl who was taken captive in Syria said to her mistress, "If only my master would see the prophet who is in Samaria! He would cure him of his leprosy." Naaman went to his master and told him what the girl from Israel had said. By all means, "Go," the King of Syria replied, "I will send a letter to the king of Israel." So Naaman left, taking with him ten talents of silver, six thousand shekels of gold and ten sets of clothing. 2 Kings 3-4 (NIV) It took faith for this young girl to approach Naaman. But God was up to something. There was a young girl who would have insight and discernment to help Naaman locate his miracle. Has there ever been a time in your life where you felt the need to say something to someone but hesitated because it didn't make sense? Stepping out on faith is where the miracles begin.

Naaman exhibited humility. He didn't look at where this young girl came from, he had faith to trust what she said. Would you have listened to a servant that was taken captive to serve you?

Miracles Usually Don't Happen the Way We Imagine

As soon as the King of Israel read the letter, he tore his robes and said, "Am I God? Can I kill and bring back to life? Why does this fellow send someone to me to be cured of his leprosy? See how he is trying to pick a quarrel with me!" 2 Kings 5:7 (NIV)

The king became angry and defensive because he couldn't cure Naaman. Maybe the king was frustrated because he didn't have a relationship with God and couldn't heal lepers?

Once again being obedient, Naaman went to the Prophet Elisha's house. When he got there, Elisha sent a messenger to tell him to go wash himself in the Jordan River seven times. Naaman was enraged. (Verse10) Was it because his expectation of how God should work was crushed? Like Naaman, I would have been disappointed too. He was probably "expecting" to be healed personally by the Prophet Elisha. Have you ever noticed that answered prayers and miracles don't happen how we picture them? Finally, it was Naaman's servants that convinced him to do like Elisha told him. After he dipped himself, he was restored like a young boy (2 Kings 5:13-14).

Faith without works is dead (James 2:26). We all can agree that having faith takes perseverance and strength. We sometimes get discouraged. The biggest point to take away from Naaman is, he wasn't prideful, he listened to his servants. Dipping seven times in the Jordan River as opposed to someone praying over him or laying hands on him wasn't what Naaman expected. However, the simple method of this miracle performed without the prophet there, did give God the credit! It was obvious that the healing came from God rather than from the sort of magical expectation that perhaps Naaman had anticipated. God received the glory!

Faith requires that we never give up. Is there something that you've given up on? A dream, a promise from God? Imagine if Naaman had stopped at six dips in the Jordan

River instead of seven? What if God healed him after the first dip because of Naaman's faith and obedience? Sometimes God is testing our obedience. Like He tested Abraham when he was asked to sacrifice his son Isaac. There was a ram in the bush! Let's stop believing that miracles won't happen because our prayers have not been answered yet within our timing. Because of God's unconditional love, He only wants what's best for us. He may not come when we want him, but He's always on time.

Prayer

> **Open my eyes oh Lord to see not just with my physical eyes. Oh God, give me 20/20 spiritual vision so that I can see clearly. Faith requires that I walk by faith and not by sight. Give me the courage to take this journey with You O Lord. In Jesus' name!**

Reflection

Faith requires that we never give up. Is there something that you've given up on.

WEEK #7

The Wrestling Match has already Been Won

Matthew 17:20 (NIV)

He replied, "Because you have so little faith. Truly I tell you, if you have faith as small as a mustard seed, you can say to this mountain, 'Move from here to there,' and it will move. Nothing will be impossible for you."

Faith is a familiar work. However, when we're faced with a situation that requires us to put our faith into action, we sometimes find ourselves in a wrestling match. Faith is often thought of as a thing we have - a belief in something or someone. The Bible tells us to "fight the good fight of faith." 1 Timothy 6:12 (NIV) Winning a good faith-wrestling match can even make you stronger.

Some of the strongest and most influential people in the Bible struggled with faith. Don't be surprised when your faith is challenged to a wrestling match. Here are three people who wrestled with faith. Being a disciple of Jesus doesn't automatically make us a faith giant.

Thomas became known as "Doubting Thomas" because he wrestled with the truth that Jesus rose from the dead. John 20:25

Jacob wrestled with the angel and did not let go until he was blessed (Genesis 32:22-32 NIV).

David was known as a man after God's own heart, yet David was no stranger to wrestling with his faith. The book of Psalm is full of his questioning and pain, as well as his victories.

There are ways we can win our wrestling match with faith. We must remove the doubt by sticking with what we know. It is very important that we remind ourselves of God's promises and prayers He's answered in our lives, and our personal history with Him. These thoughts can quiet the raging questions of what if, what about, and why. Lastly, let's have faith like a child reaching out to a parent when they're scared. When we choose to reach out to God through prayer and worship, we are reminded that He's bigger than our opponent.

Sometimes we need to ask for prayer or seek the counsel of a friend or pastor. There's no shame in getting help. We are the body of Christ. Building each other up is what we're called to do.

Our wrestling match has already been won. Be prepared to share your victory!

Prayer

> **I thank You in advance for the victory that has already been won. I thank You and receive the win, in faith! In Jesus' name, Amen!**

Reflection

When we choose to reach out to God through prayer and worship, we are reminded that He's bigger than our opponent.

WEEK #8

Travel Light

Matthew 11:28-30 (TPT)

"Are you weary, carrying a heavy burden? Then come to me. I will refresh your life, for I am your oasis. Simply join your life with mine. Learn my ways and you'll discover that I'm gentle, humble, easy to please. You will find refreshment and rest in me. For all that I require of you will be pleasant and easy to bear."

Have you ever over packed your suitcase for a trip? As a result of this, did you end up carrying around unnecessary weight? I have made this mistake on more than one occasion only to find out that I didn't need half of the things I packed. This is the same way we feel when we carry the burdens of the world on our shoulders. Carrying extra weight leads to depression, anxiety and feeling overwhelmed.

What are you packing unnecessarily? Is it worry, past hurt, shame, defeat, unforgiveness? Give everything to Jesus, He has enough room to store all your extra baggage. He's waiting to take all your heavy weight at no charge. Let's stop picking up what we laid down at the altar. We feel so great after a prayer, then we pick it back up five minutes later. I have been guilty of this. Trust Him, it's already done!

Trust in the Lord with all your heart, and do not lean on your own understanding. Proverbs 3:5 (NASB)

Have you ever worried about something for nothing only to find out that the problem was already resolved, and you worried for no reason? Of course, we're going to get rattled at times because we are human. However, let's remember to trust the Lord because He has already worked it out! Reflect on how He delivered you before. Use this as a reference of His goodness. If God did it before, He will do it again!

Take off the heaviness and put on the garment of praise! Unload that extra baggage and travel light!

Prayer

> **Lord, we thank You in advance for lightening our load. We lay it all at your feet. Help us to keep our focus on You and not what's going on around us. You are a God that delights in seeing His children at peace. You know what weight we're carrying. Give us the faith to trust that we don't have to carry any unnecessary weight. You carried it on the cross for our sake. In Jesus' name!**

Give everything to Jesus, He has enough room to store all your extra baggage. He's waiting to take all your heavy weight at no charge.

Behind the Veil

WEEK #9

Don't Lose Your Peace

John 16:33 (ESV)

"I have said these things to you, that in me you may have peace. In the world you will have tribulation. But take heart; I have overcome the world."

It is so important not to allow anything or anyone rob us of our peace. Unlike being robbed by a person, we have the choice not to let the enemy rob us of our peace. Taking this stand will have a major impact on experiencing the joy of the Lord. God intended for us to have peace that surpasses all understanding. It's the peace we experience even when chaos is present.

What can rob us of our peace? Is it losing sleep over something we can't control instead of resting in Jesus? Being disappointed about something that didn't work out the way we expected? Watching the news? Listening to the CDC; wear a mask today, don't wear a mask tomorrow? If we take our burdens to the Lord and leave them there, we will be at peace.

God's offer of peace is real and is not based on our feelings. I'm not saying it's always easy. However, if we make an effort and lean on our God, He will calm our storm and give us peace.

"You will keep in perfect peace, whose mind stays on You, because he trusts in you." Isaiah 26:3 (NIV)

So, what does it mean if there is no peace? Scripture reveals how God will use a lack of peace as a revelation to warn us of error or danger.

Jesus himself experienced a lack of peace as God revealed to him the reality of what he was facing just days before His crucifixion.

Jesus replied, "The hour has come for the Son of Man to be glorified... Now my soul is troubled, and what shall I say? 'Father save me from this hour'? No, it was for this very reason I came to this hour. Father, glorify your name!" John 12:23, 27, 28 (NIV)

God's peace is permanent and secure. When circumstances are free of conflict, we enjoy momentary peace. But when we face difficult relationships, health problems, and financial crisis, the momentary quiet is disrupted and chaos rules the day. Our God offers peace in the midst of chaos. His peace doesn't change with the circumstances; it is secure in spite of the circumstances. When you are tempted to think about your challenges, remember how God's desire for us is to be at peace.

"Though the mountains be shaken and the hills be removed, yet my unfailing love for you will not be shaken nor my covenant of peace be removed, says the Lord, who has compassion on you." Isaiah 54:10 (NIV)

Lacking human companionship, Paul found peace in divine fellowship. An anonymous person once said, "Peace is not the absence of conflict but the presence of God no matter what the conflict."

Prayer

I will not let anything, or anyone rob me of my peace. Lord, strengthen my relationship with You so that my mind only focuses on Your truth. Erase all the lies in my mind, in Jesus' name!

Reflection

It is so important not to allow anything or anyone rob us of our peace. Unlike being robbed by a person, we have the choice not to let the enemy rob us of our peace.

WEEK #10

What is Your Identity?

Genesis 1:27 (NIV)

So God created mankind in his own image,
in the image of God he created them."

Although discovering our true identity can be challenging, it has already been determined by God. "This world is structured in a way that we tie our identity and purpose to our jobs, families, successes, and failures. We even compare ourselves to others. When you are feeling uncertain about who God created you to be, remind yourself of who God says you are.

We have been blessed with every spiritual blessing, we have been chosen, adopted, redeemed, forgiven, grace-lavished and unconditionally loved and accepted.

It is extremely helpful to write down verses that remind you of God's words spoken about us. A good scripture to write down as a reminder is "You are God's masterpiece" found in Ephesians 2:10. A masterpiece is a one of a kind - no duplicates. We are all born with a one-of-a-kind fingerprint.

Prayer

Lord I am enough; Your Word describes who I am in you. Let me be reminded of your Words that describe your love for me. In Jesus' name, Amen!

Reflection

A masterpiece is a one of a kind - no duplicates. We are all born with a one of a kind fingerprint.

WEEK #11

Look in the Mirror

1 Samuel 16:7 (NIV)

But the Lord said to Samuel, "Do not consider his appearance or his height, for I have rejected him. The Lord does not look at the things people look at. People look at the outward appearance, but the Lord looks at the heart."

You may have heard the saying "beauty is only skin-deep, "which means that while someone may be beautiful on the outside, their character—what's inside, and more meaningful—isn't necessarily attractive.

My dad once said, "Tina, the person you see in the mirror is the person you will attract." Years later what he said made sense. He wanted me to focus on the inward person, not the outward person. Let's smile, show more love, and demonstrate compassion so that others will see Christ in us.

As in water, face reflects face, so the heart of man reflects the man. Proverbs 27:19 (ESV)

Do you have a hard time getting past what we see with our physical eyes? This world is designed to keep our minds focused on all of the negativity, division, hate, lust and the list goes on. However, sometimes when we look in the mirror, we see who we once were or who we are trying to become rather than how God sees us. Let's search ourselves inwardly. It is so easy to look great on the outside but, what do we gain if we feel horrible on the inside? Our Father wants us to experience His fullness by knowing who we are in Him. The scripture says, "God created man in His own image." Genesis 1:27 (ESV) This means we are beautiful inside and out!

An example of looking attractive on the outside and unattractive on the inside is Rebecca. Genesis 26:7 describes her as being very beautiful. However, Genesis 27 gives a highlight of Rebecca's life and her actions in the deception of her husband, Isaac. Esau was the firstborn of Isaac and Rebecca and, therefore, was entitled to the blessing. But Rebecca orchestrated a plan for her younger son, Jacob, to receive the blessing instead. Not only did this internal ugliness affect her, but it also affected her son.

Let's focus on the beauty within. When you look in the mirror, who do you see?

Prayer

> Lord, when people see me, let them see You within my heart. Let me stay focused on making certain that my heart is always connected to Your heart. When I am tempted to act out of character, guide me back to You. Thank you, Jesus.

Sometimes when we look in the mirror, we see who we once were or who we are trying to become rather than how God sees us.

WEEK #12

Becoming

Romans 12:1-2

Becoming more Christlike is the result of surrender to the Holy Spirit. This scripture says that worship involves a total self-dedication to God. We volunteer our bodies as "living sacrifices," and our minds are renewed and transformed.

In order to "become" we must leave something behind. Oftentimes, the weight of the world can prohibit us from moving forward. Have you ever felt like you've been held back from His purpose and plan for your life because you couldn't let go of the past? I love how scripture describes worship as total dedication to God. John 4:24 (NIV) says "God is spirit, and his worshippers must worship in the Spirit and in truth." When we're transparent, transformation *will* occur.

Why is it so difficult for us to transform? Is it because we feel uncomfortable when we're transforming or becoming? Is it because we feel comfortable with feeling comfortable? Here are two examples in the Bible of feeling uncomfortable: When David was "becoming" king, David encountered uncomfortable situations. When Esther was "becoming" queen, she experienced uncomfortable circumstances. The common denominator for both of them was their faith and trust in God.

Let's stay focused on how God has delivered us from our uncomfortable experiences and how He is always making a way out of no way. This transformation is for us to be all that He has called us to be!

Proverbs 3:5-6 (NIV) advises us to "Trust in the LORD with all your heart and lean not on your own understanding; in all your ways submit to Him, and He will make your paths straight."

Prayer

> Lord transform my mind, body, and spirit so that I can become the person that You called me to be. Let me continue to become more loving, more patient and more like You. In Jesus Holy name I pray, Amen!

Reflection

Let's stay focused on how God has delivered us from our uncomfortable experiences and how He is always making a way out of no way.

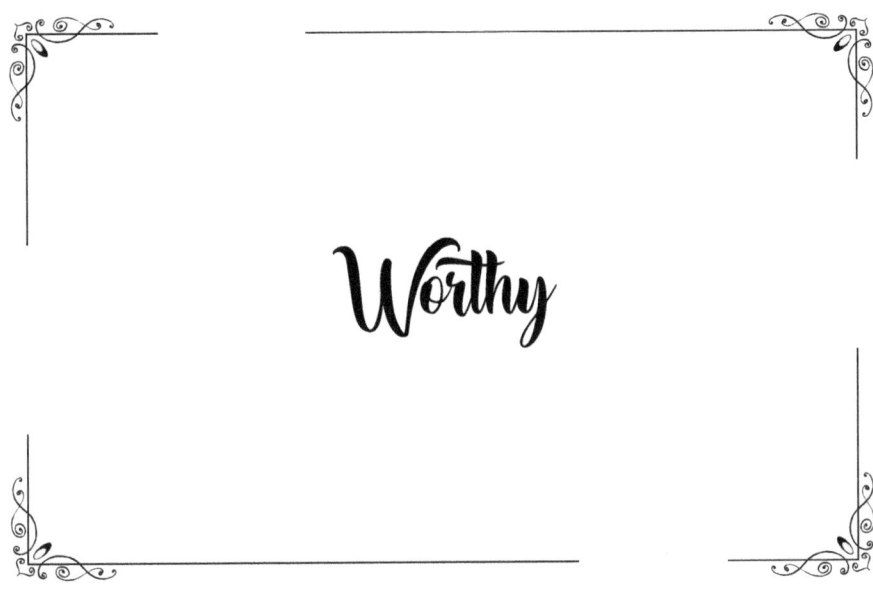

WEEK #13

What Are We Thinking About?

2 Corinthians 10:5 (KJV)

"Casting down imaginations, and every high thing that exalteth itself against the knowledge of God and bringing into captivity every thought to the obedience of Christ."

It's so easy for us to get distracted by what's going on around us. I've listed seven bible verses to help us extract negative thoughts out of our minds when we're faced with lies from the enemy. You probably have favorite Bible verses that you already rely on. We must recondition our minds daily through prayer and the word of God. I'm sure you already know this; however, reminders are very helpful.

"Keep your thoughts continually fixed on all that is authentic and real, honorable and admirable, beautiful and respectful, pure and holy, merciful and kind. And fasten your thoughts on every glorious work of God, praising him always." Philippians 4:8 (TPT)

Saying these kind words are nourishing to the soul, such as, *thank you, you're welcome, I love you, how are you?* The heart responds!

"With man this is impossible, but with God all things are possible." Matthew 19:26 (NIV) We serve a God who can do anything but fail! "Don't worry about tomorrow, for tomorrow will bring its own worries. Today's trouble is enough for today." Matthew 6:34 (NLT)

Isn't today enough? Let's not concern ourselves with what's going to happen tomorrow, doing so brings on anxiety.

All we need to know is God will make a way out of no way and He will work everything out for our good. He is miraculous, indescribable, marvelous, and victorious. He's a Healer and a way maker. Join me by adding more words to describe who He is to you!

Prayer

> **Father, cover my thoughts with reminders of Your promises. Help me to cast down all thoughts that do not line up with what Your Word says. In Jesus' name, Amen.**

Reflection

> Isn't today enough? Let's not concern ourselves with what's going to happen tomorrow, doing so brings on anxiety.

WEEK #14

Who is Your Teacher?

Luke 2:41

Jesus' parents couldn't find him for three days. Why? Because He was at the temple, sitting among teachers, both listening to them and asking them questions. All who heard him were astonished at his understanding and answers. When his parents saw him, they were amazed.

Yes, Jesus was among the teachers. He was learning from them! Are we around people that can teach us? Are we pouring out and not being poured into? If you notice, a lot of successful people have mentors and coaches. The definition of a coach is someone whose job is to teach people to improve at a sport, skill, or school subject. A coach's job is to bring out the qualities that are within a person. A football coach doesn't make the plays, he instructs and motivates the player.

Are we willing to listen to the advice of others? Do we have to always be in charge? Do things have to go our way or else it's not right? Do we have a hard time trusting others? If we answered yes to at least one of these questions, let's work on making a change. If Jesus could learn from teachers, why can't we? Notice how Jesus was sitting among the teachers both listening to them and asking them questions. Sometimes we can't learn because we're not listening. Are you guilty of interrupting someone when they're talking? I am guilty of this. We are unable to receive good advice when we're not willing to listen. The good news is, Jesus is our greatest mentor! Who is your teacher?

Prayer

> Mighty God! Give me ears to listen and learn from others. Let me teach when possible. Don't let pride get in the way of learning. I thank you God for being the best mentor and coach. Thank you, Jesus! Amen!

Sometimes we can't learn because we're not listening.

WEEK #15

Breathe

John 20:19-22 (NIV)

On the evening of that first day of the week, when the disciples were together, with the doors locked in fear of the Jewish leaders, Jesus came and stood among them and said, "Peace be with you!" After he said this, he showed them his hands and side. The disciples were overjoyed when they saw the Lord. Again, Jesus said, "Peace be with you! As the Father has sent me, I am sending you." And with that he breathed on them and said, "Receive the Holy Spirit."

The same Jesus that breathed on the disciples is the same Jesus that has breathed his Holy Spirit in us. When He breathes on us, we feel peace and joy. There's a sense of calmness that embraces our soul, it's called peace! Ask God to breathe on you, your family, your health, and your finances.

"Thus says God, the LORD, who created the heavens and stretched them out, who spread out the earth and what comes from it, who gives breath to the people on it and spirit to those who walk in it." Isaiah 42:5 (ESV)

How beautiful is this? Our Creator promises us that all we must do is walk in the spirit that He has given us. He promises to breathe on us. God is not looking for perfection, He's looking for a relationship with us.

Then he said to me, "Prophesy to the breath; prophesy, son of man, and say to it, this is what the Sovereign LORD says: Come from the four winds, O breath, and breathe into these slain, that they may live." So, I prophesied as he commanded me, and breath entered them; they came to life and stood up on their feet--a vast army. Ezekiel 37:9-10 (NIV)

Like Ezekiel, we have the power through faith and hope to speak life into a situation. Whatever may have been broken can be restored to life. When God told Ezekiel to "prophesy to the breath" he was saying "tell Israel of my promise of restoration, tell them that I will be with them and that they are not cut off from me." This is a promise that we can all hold onto, we will never be cut off by God!

Prayer

> **Breathe on me Lord like a calm wind. Breathe on my family, my mind, my health and my finances. Thank you, Jesus! Amen.**

Reflection

God is not looking for perfection, He's looking for a relationship with us.

WEEK #16

I Am Enough

1 John 3:1 (NIV)

"See what great love the Father has lavished on us, that we should be called children of God! And that is what we are! The reason the world does not know us is that it did not know him."

Do you sometimes struggle with inadequacies by thinking you are not enough for your family, job, church, or friends? Some of this stems from living in a competitive world. Social media plays a big role. People are craving for "likes" and "comments" on Facebook and Instagram. Do you wonder or doubt that you are enough? If you feel this way you are not alone with these feelings of insecurities. We are always seeking more. We are not satisfied with our accomplishments. We want more and more. The scriptures say that we should be called children of God. Isn't this enough?

Moses questioned God about being good enough. Read carefully how God responded in these two verses. Moses argued with God, revealing his insecurity: *"Who am I that I should go?"* he asked. God responded, *"I will be with you and promise to bring you to worship on this mountain."* Exodus 3:11-12 (NIV) *"What if they do not believe me or listen to me?"* God demonstrated he would use miracles and signs to show proof. Exodus 4:1-9 (NIV)

Does this sound familiar? I know I have questioned God and asked Him "who me?" And He answered and said "yes, you."

Sometimes we're waiting to feel comfortable. But guess what? We are usually going to feel uncomfortable. I love how God told Moses that He would be with him when he questioned being good enough.

The same God that assured Moses that he was good enough, is the same God that is telling you that *you* are good enough. The next time you question yourself about being good enough, remember that you are more than enough, and God is with you!

Prayer

> **Dear God when I question if I'm good enough, please let me be reminded that You are with me. I will also remember the love You have for me to be right by my side when I question if I'm good enough. Your word says I am good enough. In Jesus' name Amen.**

We are always seeking more. We are not satisfied with our accomplishments. We want more and more. The scriptures say that we should be called children of God. Isn't this enough?

Seasons of Drought

WEEK #17

Infertility

Genesis 6:9 (NIV)

"Let us not become weary in doing good, for at the proper time we will reap a harvest if we do not give up."

Is there something that you've been hoping for and dreaming of, but it hasn't happened? The key is never stop trusting God, he will bring it to life! I was in a group with several women that experienced disappointments over and over again about conceiving. The common denominator was trust. All of them felt like giving up. The other common denominator was they trusted God.

Abraham fell facedown, he laughed and said to himself, "Will a son be born to a man a hundred years old? Will Sarah bear a child at the age of ninety? Then God said, "Yes, but your wife Sarah will bear you a son, and you will call him Isaac." Genesis 17:17 and 19 (NIV) Imagine how Sarah felt when God gave her a promise at 90 years old that she would conceive a child. The Bible says that Abraham laughed, and Sarah didn't believe. Don't give up on your delayed promise! God will cause delays to strengthen our faith. In the end, Sarah's joy was her son Isaac.

Prayer

Lord give me the patience, trust, and strength to wait on You. When it doesn't make sense let me trust You. When it seems impossible let me wait on You. Increase my faith and decrease my doubt. In Jesus' name, Amen!

Reflection

Don't give up on your delayed promise! God will cause delays to strengthen our faith.

WEEK #18

He is in the Middle

John 19:18 (NLT)

"There they nailed him to the cross. Two others were crucified with him, one on either side, with Jesus between them."

Jesus sacrificed His life for us so that we do not have to bear our difficulties alone. When we acknowledge His presence in the middle of all our decisions, we will get to the end in a peaceful way.

"Being confident of this very thing, that he who hath begun a good work in you will perform it until the day of Jesus Christ." Philippians 1:6 (NKV)

There are so many middle references in our lives. For example, flying in a plane and sitting in the middle seat; in the middle of a health challenge; in the middle of a pandemic; in the middle of a wonderful project, or in the middle of a challenging situation. What is your middle? The most important thing for us to realize is, God is always with us. Sometimes being in the middle can be uncomfortable. I can't imagine the discomfort that Jesus felt in the middle of the cross bearing our sins. Next time you're in the middle of a situation, look at it as a place where you can gain strength and build your faith. There is nothing too hard for our God to handle. His desire is to give us peace in the middle!

Joshua set up the twelve stones that had been in the middle of the Jordan River at the spot where the priests who carried the Ark of the Covenant had stood. And they are there to this day. Joshua 4:9 (NIV)

The middle can symbolize where we've come from, where we are and where we're going. As a reminder of God's greatness, Joshua marked his middle with stones. How will you mark your middle to remind you of God's greatness? The next time you're faced with a challenging situation, look at it as an opportunity to create a landmark that leads to a testimony!

Prayer

> **Mighty God! We thank you in advance for giving us the strength needed to accomplish what You have planned for us in the middle. Strengthen our faith, in Jesus' name, Amen!**

Reflection

Next time you're in the middle of a situation, look at it as a place where you can gain strength and build your faith.

WEEK #19

Obey When it Doesn't Make Sense

Psalms 128:1 (TPT)

"How joyous are those who love the Lord and bow low before God, ready to obey him."

Obedience is one of the main components of our relationship with God. We must trust God and have faith that all things work together for our good. Romans 8:28. If we do not obey Him there will be consequences. Do we partially obey God by adding our own meaning to something and wonder why things are not working out? Keep in mind that when we obey Him it's not always going to make sense. Did it make sense to Noah when he built the ark? It wasn't raining. Or when the Lord told Moses to stretch out his hand and the Red Sea was parted? What about when Moses saw the burning bush and God commanded him to take off his sandals? "Do not come any closer, God said. Take off your Sandals, for the place where you are standing is holy ground." Exodus 3:5 (NIV) Would it make sense for you to take off your shoes when flames were surrounding you? Moses, in his disgust and anger at Israel's sins and rebellion, disobeyed God and struck the rock twice, instead of speaking to it. Numbers 20:11 (NIV) We must obey God, even when it doesn't make sense.

Did Joshua question God in Joshua 3:8-9 (NIV)? "Tell the priests who carry the ark of the covenant: 'When you reach the edge of the Jordan's waters, go and stand in the river.'"

Joshua said to the Israelites, "Come here and listen to the words of the Lord your God." Joshua was obedient even when it didn't make sense.

When God commands us to do something, let's not partially obey Him by altering his instructions so that it makes sense to us. We must trust and obey Him fully and wait. A good example of not trusting and obeying God was the Israelites. Unfortunately, for Moses, one act of disobedience caused him not to enter the Promised Land. "Walk in obedience to him, and keep his decrees and commands, his laws and regulations, as written in the Law of Moses. Do this so that you may prosper in all you do and wherever you go." 1 Kings 2:3 (NIV)

Let's stop waiting for life experiences to make sense before we obey. We can't lose by obeying God. Trust God and leave the consequences to Him.

Prayer

> **Lord increase my faith so that I can trust You when things don't make sense to me. Let me lean not on my understanding by rationalizing or concerning myself with things that You've already taken care of. I believe the more that I do this, the more I will trust You. In Jesus' name, I pray.**

Let's stop waiting for life experiences to make sense before we obey. We can't lose by obeying God. Trust God and leave the consequences to Him.

WEEK #20

Isaiah 40:31 (TPT)

"But those who wait for Yahweh's grace will experience divine strength. They will rise up on soaring wings and fly like eagles, run their race without growing weary and walk-through life without giving up."

Did you play or watch someone play jump rope? If you did, do you remember how you had to wait for the right timing to jump in? It took courage to jump in. Waiting is not easy. "Wait on the LORD; be of good courage, and He shall strengthen thine heart: wait, I say, on the LORD." Psalms 27:14 (KJV)

Abraham was promised an heir through his wife Sarah despite her old age. This period of waiting lasted 25 years. Sarah did eventually give birth to Isaac "and the Lord did for Sarah as he had promised." Genesis 21:1 (NIV)

Joseph patiently worked faithfully in every situation he found himself in. He waited for God to fulfill His promise that Joseph would be a leader of his people. Genesis 37:5-11. Job waited through suffering. David waited to be king at the appointed time. Hannah waited for Samuel. And the most important wait – Jesus; He waited to begin His ministry. His ministry started at the age of thirty years old. If you're waiting on something, don't give up. I am convinced that o God will fully satisfy every need you have, for I have seen the abundant riches of glory revealed to me through the Anointed One, Jesus Christ! Philippians 4:19. Don't be discouraged!

"Have I not commanded you? Be strong and courageous. Do not be afraid; do not be discouraged, for the LORD your God will be with you wherever you go." Joshua 1:9 (NIV)

It takes courage to wait regardless of our circumstances. While we're waiting, the enemy will whisper lies to us like, "it's too late," "you're too old or young," "you're not good enough." The Devil is a liar! We must remain steadfast. Continue to wait, it's never too late for us to receive the promises that our Father has for us.

Prayer

> Dear God, give me the patience and courage while I wait for the great things that You have planned for me. Let me jump in at the right time by learning to hear Your voice. Let your timing be my timing. Thank you, Lord!

It takes courage to wait regardless of our circumstances. While we're waiting, the enemy will whisper lies to us like, "it's too late," "you're too old or young," "you're not good enough."

Panicked and Paralyzed

WEEK #21

How Are You Prioritizing Your Time?

Exodus 18:17-21, 24 (NIV)

"Moses' father-in-law replied, "What you are doing is not good. You and these people who come to you will only wear yourselves out. The work is too heavy for you; you cannot handle it alone. Listen now to me and I will give you some advice, and may God be with you. You must be the people's representative before God and bring their disputes to him. Teach them his decrees and instructions, and show them the way they are to live and how they are to behave. But select capable men from all the people—men who fear God, trustworthy men who hate dishonest gain—and appoint them as officials over thousands, hundreds, fifties and tens." Moses listened to his father-in-law and did everything he said."

Prioritizing our time can sometimes be difficult. Moses's father-in-law helped him by advising him to prioritize his time. He told Moses that he couldn't do everything alone. I'm sure listening to his father-in-law took away a lot of stress. Moses was working himself to the bones. What's the old saying "work smart and not hard." Let's remember that we can't do everything alone, it leads to exhaustion and sometimes resentment. Do we take on tasks alone because we do not trust that someone else can do something as good as us? Or do we feel if we ask for help, someone might think we're not smart enough? Ask yourself, *"is there something that someone can help me with today?"* Asking for help is humbling and makes others feel valued. Even children love to help.

Setting aside a place and time to meet God is like going on vacation or a spa day; it's so relaxing! You can meet him with a cup of coffee or tea and your Bible. The good thing is you can just wait for him to talk to you. Do you have a prayer closet, or a place set aside to meet Jesus every morning? The movie *War Room* is what comes to mind. Priscilla Shirer created a place to pray in a closet.

"But seek ye first his kingdom, and his righteousness; and all these things shall be added unto you." Matthew 6:33 (NIV)

Continue to make time for God first every day. Although tempting, let's try not to check emails or social media before talking to our Father. When we start our day off by putting God first, we will feel at peace. I'm not saying we won't encounter some challenges, but we will go through them better. "Evening, and morning, and at noon, will I pray, and cry aloud: and he shall hear my voice." Psalm 55:17 (KJV) Try your best to prioritize your time.

Prayer

> **Lord help me to put You first in everything that I do. Help me to realize that I can't do everything alone. I thank You for the people that You have placed in my life that are willing to assist me before I become overwhelmed. I tell pride to leave in the mighty name of Jesus!**

Reflection

Let's remember that we can't do everything alone, it leads to exhaustion and sometimes resentment.

WEEK #22

Angels Are Watching Over Us!

Read Matthew 18:10 (NIV)

Every child is constantly under the watchful care of guardian angels. Jesus Christ implies when he tells his disciples about children in "See that you do not despise one of these little ones. For I tell you that their angels in heaven always see the face of my Father in heaven."

What if we had someone who was assigned to us every day to help us? Guess what? There is someone assigned to us personally. It's our guardian angel.

Guardian angels. I often think about whether children and babies are aware of their angels. They laugh and smile when they're asleep. If we thought about angels more, we wouldn't be as fearful.

Thinking about angels can stir up such a peaceful feeling. How often do you think about angels? Who are angels and why were they created? God created angels for his purpose. Their primary duty is to serve and worship him. They go between heaven and earth for us! They are watchers. Genesis (33:2) Angels never rest! Isn't it good to know that we are protected?

Angels are mighty created spiritual beings. For some reason they are viewed and described as small, cute, cuddly beings. One angel took down an army. One night the angel of the Lord went out and put to death 185,000 people in the Assyrian camp. When the people got up the next morning, there were dead bodies. King 19:35 (NIV) Why are we concerned or worried about what has or can happen to us? We are protected.

Daniel is an example of being protected many times by angels. Daniel encountered two archangels. God sent his angel in the lion's den. Daniel 6:22

Did you know that God made us lower than angels? Hebrews 2:7 Do not forget to show hospitality to strangers, for by so doing some people have shown hospitality to angels without knowing it. Hebrew 13:2 (NIV) We must be very careful when we're talking to people regardless of their differences. What if it's an angel? We are never alone; angels are watching over us day and night.

Prayer

> Lord, we thank you for dispatching your angels from heaven to protect us. It is so comforting to know that they never sleep. How reassuring to know that we are loved so much until you assigned angels to protect me. Thank you, Jesus!

Reflection

One angel took down an army.

WEEK #23

Tell the Mountain to Move

Matthew 17:20 (NIV)

"He replied, "Because you have so little faith. Truly I tell you, if you have faith as small as a mustard seed, you can say to this mountain, 'Move from here to there,' and it will move. Nothing will be impossible for you."

Is our faith getting in the way of moving our mountain? What is your mountain? Is it your health? Anxiety? Depression? Loss? Fear? Unforgiveness? Have you moved a mountain lately? Or was it an answered prayer? Have you witnessed healing? I have! God recently moved my brother's mountain. His mountain was cancerous, and it was removed through prayer. Even if you do not see your mountain being moved, have confidence that it is being moved. It is necessary for us to have faith in others until they are strong enough to have faith on their own. I'm reminded of the three men that made a hole in the roof and lowered their friend where Jesus was. God healed the man because of his friends' faith. (Luke 5:19)

Mountains do not move – that is just the point. They are the ultimate symbol of stability. So, when Jesus speaks of mountains being moved, or even more dramatically thrown into the sea, as the result of faithful prayer, in Matthew 17:20; 21:21, he is deliberately invoking a human impossibility.

Sarah's mountain was infertility. Moses's mountain was his stuttering speech. Paul's mountain was the thorn in his side.

Gideon's mountain was fear. Elijah's mountain was Jezebel. David's mountain was lust. What is your mountain? Tell it to move!

Mountains come in different sizes and are there to cover us from the elements. They can also hide us from danger. The cave is where David went. Jesus went to the mountain to pray. Moses wrote the Ten Commandments on a mountain.

If our Lord can heal a blind man, cause a deaf man to hear, heal the woman with the issue of blood, make the lame walk, and raise Lazarus from the dead; He can move our mountain!

Prayer

> **Today I am commanding my mountain to move in the Mighty name of Jesus! Nothing is too great for my God. You make the impossible happen. You are the God that can cause the earth to tremble. In Jesus' name I pray, Amen.**

Reflection

> Even if you do not see your mountain being moved, have confidence that it is being moved.

WEEK #24

Slow Down

Jeremiah 2:25 (MSG)

"Slow down. Take a deep breath. What's the hurry? Why wear yourself out? Just what are you after anyway?"

During a recent visit with my ten-year-old granddaughter Olivia, she expressed her viewpoint about why tortoises live up to two hundred years. She said "Grantee, tortoises live longer because they take their time and do not rush, they use very little energy." What a revelation! As human beings we are always in a hurry. We use way too much unnecessary energy.

Rushing makes us feel anxious and oftentimes causes us to make rash decisions. How can we have peace if we're moving fast? Slow down! I have to sometimes tell myself to walk slowly because I find myself rushing for no reason. Doing so, sometimes causes me to feel irritable and anxious. Can you relate to this? "Careful planning puts you ahead in the long run; hurry and scurry puts you further behind." Proverbs 21:5 (MSG)

Let's ask God for insight when we create our schedules and move at a pace that pleases Him. Let's be wise so that we can avoid the trap of rushing, which often leads us in the wrong direction. When we pray and ask for God's insight, we are able to meet our deadlines with ease.

That is the focus Jesus had as He walked through the crowd toward Jairus' house. And yet, He must have walked slowly enough to feel the touch of one woman in the crowd. Unbelievable balance, wouldn't you say? Would He have felt her touch if He was walking swiftly? I'm just making a point. We know that fast or slow, Jesus feels our touch.

When God created us, He did so in a precise, strategic manner. Do you think that He was in a hurry? Or did He take His time to create us all uniquely? We rush out of the house, we respond to text messages in a hurry, sometimes responding incorrectly. Have you ever sent a text message quickly and was embarrassed because your text didn't make any sense? I am guilty of doing this. We dash off to a meeting, we rush to board a plane. Slow down! I love playing golf because I'm forced to slow down. The next time we are tempted to rush, let's sound off the alarm in our heads by saying, slow down!

Prayer

> Lord guide my footsteps, plan my schedule, calm my mind so that I can slow down when making decisions and most importantly so I can hear from You.

Reflection

> Let's ask God for insight when we create our schedules and move at a pace that pleases Him.

Battlefield of the Mind

WEEK #25

Battlefield of the Mind

2 Corinthians 10:5 (NIV)

"We demolish arguments and every pretension that sets itself up against the knowledge of God, and we take captive every thought to make it obedient to Christ."

Do you sometimes feel like your thoughts take you to a place where you don't want to go? Well, you're not alone; this happens to all of us. The Bible says take captive to every thought to make it obedient to Christ. This means to gain control over what we think about. In other words, we have to hold those negative thoughts hostage. We have to fight! Is there something that you're battling with in your mind today? A great scripture to read is, "I know what it means to lack, and I know what it means to experience overwhelming abundance. For I'm trained in the secret of overcoming all things, whether in fullness or in hunger. And I find that the strength of Christ's explosive power infuses me to conquer every difficulty." Philippians 4:12-13 (TPT)

When thoughts occur that are negative, we have to pull out our swords. "For the word of God is alive and active. Sharper than any double-edged sword, it penetrates even to divide soul and spirit, joints and marrow; it judges the thoughts and attitudes of the heart." Hebrews 4:12 (NIV)

Satan can't read minds. Since Satan is not divine, he is not omniscient. Only God knows your thoughts before you think them. However, the enemy will fool you to make you think that he can read your mind. He's the father of lies!

Satan also wants to take from you and destroy your peace. But we can fight back the way Jesus did. When Jesus was tempted by Satan, He used Scripture to counter him each time. He knew that Satan couldn't win against the ultimate truth of God's Word. If Jesus, the Son of God, used Scripture to fight temptation, we can do the same in our thought lives.

"Have I not commanded you? Be strong and courageous. Do not be frightened, and do not be dismayed, for the Lord your God is with you wherever you go." Joshua 1:9 (NIV)

Joshua won the battle in his mind before he defeated the land of Canaan. The spies that went before him were defeated in their minds because they saw giants. Joshua saw grasshoppers! How are we positioning our thoughts? What do you see when the battle time comes? Are we letting disappointments or fear to influence our thoughts? "For the Spirit God gave us does not make us timid, but gives us power, love and self-discipline." 2 Timothy 1:7 (NIV)

Prayer

Lord, we pray today that we do not wrestle with our thoughts. Instead, let's continue to trust God! Don't give up because you can't see the victory. The battle was won on the cross. The victory is ours! In Jesus' name, Amen.

Reflection

> Joshua won the battle in his mind before he defeated the land of Canaan.

WEEK #26

Training for Battle

Ephesians 6:11-12 (TPT)

"Put on God's complete set of armor provided for us, so that you will be protected as you fight against the evil strategies of the accuser! Your hand-to-hand combat is not with human beings, but with the highest principalities and authorities operating in rebellion under the heavenly realms. For they are a powerful class of demon-gods and evil spirits that hold this dark world in bondage."

You can train physically to become stronger and gain more endurance but in order to be a soldier, you need to be trained by someone with authority over you. That someone is Christ Jesus. God has given us a specific plan on how to train for battle in the book of Ephesians. Scripture says we must put on the whole armor of God. This includes covering every part of our bodies. These pieces are described as the belt of truth, breastplate of righteousness, shoes with the preparation of the gospel of peace, shield of faith, helmet of salvation, and the sword of the spirit/word of God.

Basic training is the first step in preparing you to be a soldier. God teaches us how to fight in a spiritual way and not a physical way. We must learn not to fight in the flesh. When we fight spiritually, we will win the battle the right way. The truth will break down barriers. God will sometimes allow the enemy to get close. Just don't let him gain position. We train for battle by becoming more like God. Faith is what protects us. We have to preach and declare faith. We have to declare it! Jesus didn't argue with people, He gave them the truth.

We can't have spiritual casualties of war - we have to win by using the word of God. This is how we prepare and win the battle that has already been won!

Prayer

> Lord, prepare my mind, body, and soul for any spiritual battle that comes my way. You are going before me to fight all of my battles. In Jesus' Holy name, Amen!

We train for battle by becoming more like God. Faith is what protects us.

WEEK #27

Are You Facing Your Giant?

1 Samuel 17:49 (ESV)

"And David put his hand in his bag and took out a stone and slung it and struck the Philistine on his forehead. The stone sank into his forehead, and he fell on his face to the ground."

As a child, God prepared David to become king because He knew that David would be faced with giants his entire life. I love how David's strength started with being a Shepherd Boy. He worked as a courier delivering food to his brothers. This would be referred to as DoorDash or Uber Eats nowadays. Little did he know, these were all necessary traits for being a great servant leader. David's faith was so strong that he was willing to believe that the Lord would go with him and enable him to defeat Goliath. The same God who was with David, is the same God who has already fought our battles.

"Your servant has killed both lions and bears; and this uncircumcised Philistine shall be like one of them, since he has defied the armies of the living God." David said, "The Lord, who saved me from the paw of the lion and from the paw of the bear, will save me from the hand of this Philistine." So, Saul said to David, "Go, and may the Lord be with you!" 1 Samuel 17:36–37 (NIV)

I love how David reflected on his victories. He reminded Saul that God delivered him from the bear and the lion. What has

God delivered you or is currently delivering you from? Your Goliath could be a challenge that you are praying about. Just remember the victory has been won! When we look back and remember where God has brought us from, our faith is strengthened. David had a slingshot and a rock. What is your defense? God equips us differently. He equipped David with five stones that he picked up on his way to defeat Goliath. 1 Samuel 17:40. The defense is the word of God!

David fastened on his sword over the tunic and tried walking around, because he was not used to them. "I cannot go in these," he said to Saul, "because I am not used to them." So he took them off. 1 Samuel 17:39 (NIV) Don't miss this point. Saul tried to give David "his" armor to fight the giant. David said I can't go in these. God has specifically given us our own armor. Don't wear someone else's armor, you might lose the battle! What has God equipped you with?

Prayer

> **Lord help me realize the armor You have specifically given me. Give me courage to face all of my difficulties with the greatest armor, Your word. In Jesus' name, Amen.**

Reflection

God has specifically given us our own armor. Don't wear someone else's armor, you might lose the battle!

WEEK #28

Undefeated

Romans 8:37 (NIV)

"No, in all these things we are more than conquerors through him who loved us."

Joshua was undefeated and served first as a major subordinate to Moses and then as his successor as leader of the Israelites. As such, he endured the events of the Exodus out of Egypt and spied on behalf of Moses. He then commanded the Israelites in their first battle against the Amalekites, in which Joshua triumphed.

According to the Bible, none other than God selected Joshua as Moses's successor, which is pretty much the ultimate endorsement for any leader. Joshua won his greatest and most celebrated victory by taking Jericho after his army blew down the city's walls with their trumpets. Joshua even managed to defeat the Amorite kings at Gibeon thanks to divine intervention. In this case, God made the Sun stand still so that the battle could go on for a bit longer during daylight.

In today's time who comes to mind is Andre Ward, a retired undefeated boxer. Andre is not just known for his undefeated title in boxing, he is known as "S.O.G" (Son of God) What's most impressive about Andre is his faith in God.

When God is placed first in our lives, we will live a life of victory. Our stance is what makes us undefeated.

Prayer

My King, I thank you for the victory that has already been won for me. I thank You for going before me to fight all of my battles. I serve an undefeated God. I am an overcomer in Jesus' name!

Reflection

When God is placed first in our lives, we will live a life of victory. Our stance is what makes us undefeated.

No More Shackles

WEEK #29

Let's Keep the Grave Clothes Off

John 11:44 (NIV)

"The dead man came out, his hands and feet wrapped with strips of linen, and a cloth around his face. Jesus said to them, 'Take off the grave clothes and let him go.'"

Grave clothes are the garments that hinder our spiritual and emotional lives. Our grave clothes symbolize our unbelief. Have you ever put on the wrong outfit and felt uncomfortable? Maybe we're wearing grave clothes. Wearing grave clothes can be a result of not forgiving ourselves, thinking we could have made better choices, shame, and feelings of unworthiness. These are just a few things that can keep us from experiencing the freedom that God has called us to enjoy. When we worship and praise God the grave clothes come off!

Did Jesus sacrifice His life, wear human flesh for us to live a life of bondage and defeat? He died on the cross for our sins and rose on the third day to set us free! God sacrificed His only son so that we could live a life of freedom. We may not be wearing grave clothes but may know someone else that is. Help your friends pick out a new outfit by pointing them to Jesus. "He himself bore our sins" in his body on the cross, so that we might die to sins and live for righteousness; "by his wounds you have been healed." 1 Peter 2:24 (NIV)

Prayer:

Dear God, let me choose the outfit of life and not death. You conquered the grave so that I can live a life of freedom. I thank You for Your unconditional love!

Reflection

We may not be wearing grave clothes but may know someone else that is. Help your friends pick out a new outfit by pointing them to Jesus.

WEEK #30

Let's Change our Perspective

Colossians 3:2 (TPT)

"Yes, feast on all of the treasures of the heavenly realm and fill your thoughts with heavenly realities, and not with the distractions of the natural realm."

Our true perspective comes from faith and our trust in God. Are we looking at the glass half empty or half full? The situation may not change, however, changing our perspective will give us peace of mind. Here are a few bible verses and thoughts that can be used to assist us with changing our perspective:

A loss: When one door closes another door opens. I believe that God has something better for me. Revelation 3:8 (ESV) reveals "I know your works. Behold, I have set before you an open door, which no one is able to shut. I know that you have but little power, and yet you have kept my word and have not denied my name."

Financial challenges: My situation is changing even though I can't see it. Psalms 50:10 says, "For every animal of the forest is mine, and the cattle on a thousand hills."

Health problems: God is healing me right now! Jeremiah 33:6 (NIV) confirms "Nevertheless, I will bring health and healing to it; I will heal my people and will let them enjoy abundant peace and security."

Disappointment: Disappointments are not meant to destroy me; they are meant to strengthen me. Psalm 119:116 (NIV) affirms "Sustain me, my God, according to your promise, and I will live; do not let my hopes be dashed."

David changed his perspective when his son he fathered with Bathsheba died. 2 Samuels 22-24 (NIV) He answered, "While the child was still alive, I fasted and wept. I thought, 'Who knows? The Lord may be gracious to me and let the child live.' But now that he is dead, why should I go on fasting? Can I bring him back again? I will go to him, but he will not return to me." "Then David comforted his wife Bathsheba, and he went to her and made love to her." She gave birth to a son, and they named him Solomon. David's circumstance didn't change, however, his perspective did.

Most importantly, it was Jesus' perspective that changed the world. Luke 22:42 (NKJV) declares "Father, if it is Your will, take this cup away from Me; nevertheless not My will, but Yours, be done."

Today, when we're faced with a difficult situation or a decision that has to be made; let's change our perspective.

Prayer

> **Lord help us to realize that it's not the problem, but it's the right perspective that we need to focus on. The right perspective is You! Thank you, in Jesus' name.**

Are we looking at the glass half empty or half full? The situation may not change, however, changing our perspective will give us peace of mind.

WEEK #31

Early in the Morning

Proverbs 8:17 (NIV)

"I love them that love me; and those that seek me early shall find me."

This scripture is so beautiful. Doesn't this sound like God is waiting to hear from us? Are you an early riser? Have you heard the old saying "the early bird catches the worm?" Your early could be later or earlier than mine. When we seek God first, it is easier to get through the day. However, if we do not seek Him early in the day; He is still there for us. He's such a loving God. The purpose of seeking God early or in the morning is so that we do not get distracted by the things that are going on around us. Since the morning is from midnight to noon, regardless of our schedules, we can seek Him first.

Another advantage of seeking God early is the quietness that is present. If meeting with God is challenging every morning because of your schedule, perhaps you can set aside one day a week with a cup of coffee or tea and your journal to summarize your week with Him. Psalm 5:3 (ESV) says "O Lord, in the morning you hear my voice; in the morning I prepare a sacrifice for you and watch". David's faith was so strong. He "watched" for his blessings. He knew that they were coming. What are you asking God for? Keep seeking Him early and like David, watch for your blessing.

Prayer

Lord, I pray that I see Your blessings everywhere that I go; in the grocery store, in my job, in waiting not knowing what's next. Let me believe that Your mercies are new every day. In Jesus' Holy name, Amen.

Reflection

The purpose of seeking God early or in the morning is so that we do not get distracted by the things that are going on around us.

WEEK #32

One Touch

Luke 8:43-48 (TPT)

"In the crowd that day was a woman who had suffered greatly for twelve years from slow bleeding. Even though she had spent all that she had on healers, she was still suffering. Pressing in through the crowd, she came up behind Jesus and touched the fringe of his garment. Instantly her bleeding stopped and she was healed. Jesus suddenly stopped and said to his disciples, "Someone touched me. Who was it?" While they all denied it, Peter pointed out, "Master, everyone is touching you, trying to get close to you. The crowds are so thick we can't walk through all these people without being jostled." Jesus replied, "Yes, but I felt power surge through me. Someone touched me to be healed, and they received their healing." When the woman realized she couldn't hide any longer, she came and fell trembling at Jesus' feet. Before the entire crowd she declared, "I was desperate to touch you, Jesus, for I knew if I could just touch even the fringe of your garment I would be healed." Jesus responded, "Beloved daughter, your faith in me released your healing. You may go with my peace."

This is a miracle that most of us are familiar with. Here are three points that stood out for me.

1. This woman took a chance by making herself known. With this type of condition, it was unheard of to be seen in public; in those days, women were looked down upon

and labeled as unclean. Notice how she slipped from behind him. In other words, she was hiding. Was she crawling through the crowd to get to Jesus? How could she touch the edge of His garment if she was standing? I can't imagine the courage and faith it took to press through that large crowd. He instantly healed the woman. Does this mean that we do not have faith if we're not healed instantly? No, this woman waited twelve years. What it does mean is, we can't give up no matter what!

2. She was so accustomed to hiding from people, instinctively she hid from Jesus. If we are not careful, we can find ourselves isolated from people because of shame, fear, and unworthiness. What Jesus did for this woman, He has already done for us. All it takes is one touch of faith. What are you hiding from? Are we willing to push through no matter what? God is waiting for our touch of faith.

3. Jesus called her daughter. This is how He viewed her. He knew she was coming. How can we be a daughter without a father? When we are separated from our earthly father, we can always depend on our Heavenly Father. We are His daughters; He is our daddy. He is waiting for our touch of faith.

I don't know what your issue is. What I do know is, if we take our issue to our Father, He is waiting to heal us spiritually, mentally, and physically. Just touch the hem of His garment and you will be made whole. It doesn't matter how large the crowd is, He's waiting for our touch of faith.

Prayer

Thank You for the invitation to come to You at any time. All I need is one touch from You and I know that I will be spiritually, mentally and physically made whole. It doesn't matter what the situation is, I believe that You are there for me. In Jesus' name!

Reflection

The purpose of seeking God early or in the morning is so that we do not get distracted by the things that are going on around us.

_____
_____
_____
_____
_____
_____
_____
_____
_____
_____
_____
_____
_____
_____

WEEK #33

The Lord's Prayer

Two versions of The Lord's Prayer are in the Bible:
Matthew 6:9-15 (KJV) and Luke 11:1-4 (KJV)

The prayer is the pattern for prayer Jesus taught His followers. Praying this prayer helps to approach God in prayer.

He said to them, when you pray say: Our Father who art in heaven, hallowed be your name: Thank him, give him the glory because he is the King of Kings and Lord of Lords. **Your kingdom come; your will be done on earth as it is in heaven:** Pray God's will over your life. Lord let my will line up with your will over my life. **Give us today our daily bread:** Bread is one of the most powerful symbols in the bible. Bread represents God's word, the necessities of life, it's our spiritual food. We depend on God for all of our needs. **And forgive us of our sins as we forgive those who trespass against us:** Pray for forgiveness. We must repent, Lord forgive me for anything that I've done that is unpleasant in your sight. We must also forgive others. **And lead us not into temptation but deliver us from all that is evil:** Pray for Protection. Lord, we pray for our families, children, spouses, co-workers, and the government. We pray for good health. **For yours is the kingdom and the power and the glory forever Amen:** Remind yourself that it all belongs to Him.

Prayer

Lord my money, my time, my possessions, and everything belong to You. Give me a heart to share. You are the source of all things and I thank You! In Jesus' name, Amen!

WEEK #34

Are you Hoping for Something that Hasn't Happened Yet?

Philippians 4:19-20 (TPT)

"I am convinced that my God will fully satisfy every need you have, for I have seen the abundant riches of glory revealed to me through the Anointed One, Jesus Christ!"

Are we convinced that God will fully satisfy our needs? Sometimes, we're asking for our needs to be supplied and wondering why God is taking so long. Is it because we're not totally convinced? The *Cambridge Dictionary* refers to the word convinced as being "certain about something." We must believe that God is adjusting our hearts and minds to receive the beautiful something that we have been waiting for. I believe He is lining up the right timing, situation, and people on your behalf. If we receive something too soon; it can be a loss not a gain because we're not fully prepared or ready. He loves us so much and wants to make certain that we receive His full promise at the right time. He is such a good Father who never gives up on us. He steps outside of time.

"So, we are convinced that every detail of our lives is continually woven together to fit into God's perfect plan of bringing good into our lives, for we are his lovers who have been called to fulfill his designed purpose." Romans 8:28 (TPT)

Once again, are we convinced? Our needs must line up with God's purpose for our lives. Are our hearts positioned in the right place to receive what God has for us? Are we grateful for the small things? Luke 16:10 (NIV) declares "Whoever can be trusted with very little can also be trusted with much, and whoever is dishonest with very little will also be dishonest with much."

What's helpful is that when we get overwhelmed and want to give up, we are reminded by the Holy Spirit that if we give up now, what we've hoped for could be one step away. Despite what we see with our natural eyes, we must believe that He's an on-time God. His timing is not our timing. Don't stop praying, hoping, and believing. It's already done! Wait on the Lord and be of good courage. He didn't bring us this far to leave us.

Prayer

> **Father God, I'm leaning on You to keep me lifted up when I fall short of being patient. Help me to trust that You have my best interest at heart. Let me not worry about tomorrow and trust You like the birds in the air. In Jesus' name!**

We must believe that God is adjusting our hearts and minds to receive the beautiful something that we have been waiting for.

WEEK #35

Reminders

Joshua 4:21-24 (NLT)

"Then Joshua said to the Israelites, "In the future your children will ask, "What do these stones mean?" Then you can tell them, "This is where the Israelites crossed the Jordan on dry ground." For the LORD your God dried up the river right before your eyes, and he kept it dry until you were across, just as he did at the Red Sea when he dried it up until we had all crossed over. He did this so all the nations of the earth might know that the LORD's hand is powerful, and so you might fear the LORD your God forever."

God knew that the children of Israel would forget how He brought them through the Red Sea. He explained that the 12 stones (one for each of the tribes of Israel) were to be a memorial declaring the mighty works of God, for their children and for their children's children. Because of God's love for the Israelites, He didn't want them to forget where they came from.

Remembering what you've achieved, whether it was small or large, can give you confidence and hope for the future. Reminders also can prevent us from making the same mistake twice. That's why the stones were very important for the children of Israel.

I challenge you today to write down twelve things that God has delivered you from. What comes to mind when you think of your twelve stones?

Prayer

> Today dear Father, let me be reminded of not just the large things but the small things that have impacted my life. Let me look beyond the difficult times and search for the hidden blessings that are around me. In Jesus' name, Amen.

Reflection

I challenge you today to write down twelve things that God has delivered you from.

WEEK #36

Speak Intentionally

Philippians 4:19 (TPT)

"I am convinced that my God will fully satisfy every need you have, for I have seen the abundant riches of glory revealed to me through Jesus Christ!"

Let's start today by speaking intentional thoughts. Why? Because we serve an intentional God. Nothing is by chance. He spoke the world into existence. Are our words keeping us from receiving all that God has planned for us? Do we truly believe that we are the head and not the tail? Let's be careful about what we say. Are we convinced that He will supply "all" of our needs? Maybe he's making adjustments to our minds and preparing for us to receive it.

If we receive something too soon it can be a loss and not a gain. Are you in position to receive what God has for you? Nothing is by chance. God spoke the world into existence. Are our words keeping us from receiving all that God has planned for us? Do we truly believe that we are the head and not the tail? Let's be careful about what we say.

Let's recalibrate our words by speaking intentionally. Like an engine needs recalibrating, so do our words.

Prayer

Lord assist me with speaking intentional words that line up with Your promises in the Bible. When I'm tempted to engage in words that serve no purpose, recalibrate my words and my thoughts. In Jesus' name.

Reflection

If we receive something too soon it can be a loss and not a gain.

An Heir

WEEK #37

What Is Your Legacy?

Read 1 Timothy and 2 Timothy

We are future ancestors. What we do today will determine the legacy that will be left behind. The only legacy that the children of Israel had was poor examples. Unfortunately, they didn't have ancestors to teach them. We are made in God's image to carry out His legacy by pouring into others. When we pour into others, we are leaving a legacy. You may think that you have nothing to offer, but you do. As Paul planted churches around the Mediterranean and converted thousands to Christianity, he realized he needed a trustworthy person to carry on after he died. He chose the zealous young disciple Timothy as his "successor."

Let's be like a river and pour into people, not a reservoir that just collects water. When we're pouring into others, we are leaving a legacy. It can be sharing a family recipe that has been passed down from a relative. Or, collecting photos of family members so that our grandparents and great grandparents can be remembered. No one leaves a lasting legacy accidentally. Legacy is something that we must intentionally choose to achieve. It happens over time and throughout our lives, and it determines what we leave behind for generations to come. Succession is important by carrying the baton. Once again, we must be intentional; It doesn't start when we're old, it starts now.

Like Paul, we must train the next generation on how to pass the baton so that they will lead intentionally. Paul taught Timothy about church leadership, including the role of a deacon, the requirements of an elder, as well as many other important lessons about operating a church. These were formally recorded in Paul's letters in 1 Timothy and 2 Timothy. Let's share our knowledge with our children, grandchildren, a friend's child, a niece, or nephew.

My question today is who is your successor? According to Proverbs 13:22 (NKJV), "A good man leaves an inheritance to his children's children." This verse keeps our life's goals, our vision and our legacy front and center when we're choosing how to use our money today. When we weigh what we want now against what we really want later, we realize how temporary satisfaction pales in comparison to a legacy of purpose and generational fulfillment. An inheritance is not limited to money. It also includes godly characteristics like integrity and trustworthiness. Combining a financial inheritance with wisdom and godliness ensures that the next generation will also manage God's blessings His way for God's glory long after we've graduated to heaven.

Prayer

> **Dear Father, let me leave a legacy for my family, friends and those I come into contact with. When I make choices, let me be reminded that my legacy is important and that it will have an impact on this world. Thank you, Jesus, for choosing me!**

> An inheritance is not limited to money. It also includes godly characteristics like integrity and trustworthiness.

WEEK #38

We Are Uniquely Made

Jeremiah 1:5 (NIV)

"I chose you before I formed you in the womb; I set you apart before you were born. I appointed you a prophet to the nations."

Wouldn't it be perfect if God would send down a blueprint for each of our lives? What if, when we were born, we came with an instruction manual that He wrote out for us? A manual that would outline what we should do to follow His plan for our lives? The good news is He left us the Holy Spirit, which is the best blueprint we could ever ask for to achieve our individual purpose. "For you formed my inward parts; you knitted me together in my mother's womb." Psalms 139:13 (ESV)

Although we are all made in God's image, we could not be more different as individuals. Besides our backgrounds and upbringings, we all have different interests, personalities, and dispositions. This is what makes us unique.

"For as in one body we have many members, and the members do not all have the same function, so we, though many, are one body in Christ, and individually members one of another." Romans 12:4-5 (ESV) Through our uniqueness, God has called us to come together as one body to do His works. Most importantly, He wants us to know who we are in Him. The way we make this wonderful discovery is by

We Are Uniquely Made

spending as much time as possible with God daily through prayer and reading His word.

When we're feeling overwhelmed, declaring how God sees us strengthens our faith. When you realize your self-worth, beauty, and joy in Christ, you have the fearlessness to step into your destiny and embrace your uniqueness!

Prayer

> Lord I thank You for designing me in such a unique way. Give me the courage and faith to walk into the purpose that You have mapped out for me. Thank You for loving me. In Jesus' name, Amen.

> When we're feeling overwhelmed, declaring how God sees us strengthens our faith.

WEEK #39

Are You an Upright Person?

Read Ecclesiastes 7:11-22 (NIV)

In the book of Ecclesiastes, Solomon talks about wisdom. We love this book because it is spoken from a practical point of view. Sometimes we get so caught up in what's not important. Solomon discovered this. What do you do when you've achieved your goals and money isn't an issue? Solomon sought wisdom. Without wisdom nothing else matters. *"Wisdom is the principal thing; therefore get wisdom: and with all thy getting get understanding."* Proverbs 4:7 (NKJV) What struck me most is when Solomon said, in Ecclesiastes 7:28 (NIV),while I was still searching but not finding, I found one upright man among a thousand, but not one upright woman among them all.

Solomon tells us that an immoral woman is very dangerous to anyone and everyone. If you fear God, you do well to keep away from these immoral women. From all these immoral women that Solomon warns about, there is none that is upright. It is from these findings that he later builds a conclusion that there is no upright woman. Because in this text, he has found that a dishonest woman who traps others is dangerous and among all these dishonest women, none could indeed be upright. Ecclesiastes 7:26 (NIV)

It started with Eve who ate from the forbidden tree. Then there was Rebekah, who conspired to steal her son Jacob's birthright. Jezebel scared Elijah and he ran for his life. Delilah manipulated Samson into divulging information on where his strength came from, and the list goes on.

However, several upright women come to mind: Mary, the mother of Jesus, The Savior of the World. Deborah assisted Barak in defeating Sisera and his army. Esther freed her people by going to the King on their behalf.

When we're making choices and/or decisions; let's make certain that our actions positively affect other people.

Prayer

> **Lord help me to be an upright person in everything that I do. Let me operate in an honest way even when no one sees what I am doing. I know You see me and that You reward those that are honest and upright. Don't let pride interfere in my decision-making. This I ask in Your name, Amen.**

Reflection

When we're making choices and/or decisions; let's make certain that our actions positively affect other people.

WEEK #40

What Proof Do You Need?

Read Judges 6:11-24 (NIV)

Do you need signs as proof that God is with you? Gideon needed not one but three signs to be convinced that he could carry out God's plans to defeat the Midianites. He requested proof of God's will by three miracles: first, a sign from the Angel of the Lord, in which the angel appeared to Gideon and caused fire to shoot up out of a rock.

Gideon is an example of how we sometimes view ourselves. *"How can I be mighty if I'm fearful or doubt my faith? "How can I be mighty if I struggle with anxiety?"* Isn't it amazing how God sees the greatness in us even though we can't? No matter how strong we are, it is human nature to feel insecure about something. However, the more we stay connected to God, pray, and stay in His Word, the more confident we become. The beauty is, God sees our beginning and our end.

However, Gideon was frightened when he saw the Angel of the Lord face-to-face. (Verse 22) God said to him be at peace, do not be afraid, you shall not die. (Verse 23) Isn't this what we do? We ask God for something and when he gives it to us, we're shocked or amazed? Is it because we really didn't expect Him to answer our request so quickly?

God is so merciful. Gideon received a confirmation when he overheard a man telling his friend a dream that described Gideon overtaking the Midianite camp. Judges 8:13-15 After this dream, Gideon was convinced and confident that he could defeat the army. Are we like Gideon? Do we need signs and confirmation? It's okay if we do. We serve a God that is loving and merciful!

Then Gideon built an altar to the Lord and called it Yahweh-Shalom, which means "The Lord is Peace." (Verse 24) I believe it was Gideon's encounter with God that convinced him of God's love and loyalty. Every time we experience the majesty of God, our faith is strengthened. His mercies are new every day! How much more proof do we need?

Prayer

> Father God, help me to see Your mighty signs and wonders everywhere that we go. Let me trust You and believe that you died for our sins which is all the proof I need. When I feel doubtful, I ask that You strengthen my unbelief. In Jesus' name we pray, Amen.

No matter how strong we are, it is human nature to feel insecure about something. However, the more we stay connected to God, pray, and stay in His Word, the more confident we become.

Keep it Pushing

WEEK #41

Who is Your Firefighter?

Daniel 3:24-25 (NIV)

"Then King Nebuchadnezzar leaped to his feet in amazement and asked his advisers, "Weren't there three men that we tied up and threw into the fire?" They replied, "Certainly, Your Majesty." He said, "Look! I see four men walking around in the fire, unbound and unharmed, and the fourth looks like a son of the gods."

Have you ever experienced a situation where you were ridiculed because you stood for what was right? This was the case with the three Hebrew boys, Shadrach, Meshach, and Abednego who were thrown in the fiery furnace because of their faithfulness to God by not worshiping the King's golden idol. These boys were confident that God would save them, and He did! The wonderful part is three went in and four came out. Have you ever stepped out on faith and knew that God was with you? Maybe it wasn't a hot furnace, but it was a situation that you knew only He could deliver you from.

We serve a God that will rescue us from any situation. If you are in the fire right now, keep the faith like the Hebrew boys did, and I'm confident that you will not smell like smoke when you come out. This is what stuck with me, regardless of the outcome, they were committed to their faith; even when faced with the possibility of a painful death. "But even if he does not, we want you to know, Your Majesty, that we will not serve your gods or worship the image of gold you have set up." Daniel 3:18 (NIV)

Jesus is the ultimate Firefighter. He died on the cross to rescue us from the pits of hell! So, yes, we've been through the fire, but we don't smell like smoke! When we are faithful and stand up for what is right, God will always rescue us.

Prayer

> No matter what I'm facing, teach me to stand in what's right and have the courage to know that You will fight my battles and rescue me from everything. Let me stand in Your promise that You will rescue me! Thank you Jesus!

Reflection

When we are faithful and stand up for what is right, God will always rescue us.

WEEK #42

Shout a Little Louder

Read Joshua 6:1-27

Today's devotion reminds us that following God's instructions will enable us to conquer any battle that we face. The children of Israel were on their way to the Promised Land, a land filled with milk and honey when they faced a huge obstacle, the wall of Jericho. Doesn't this sound familiar? I don't know about you but when I'm getting close to something that has been promised to me or approaching a win, for some reason there seems to be a roadblock somewhere, somehow. This was the case for the Israelites. However, because Joshua followed God's instructions the walls fell, and they crossed over.

First, the strategy was laid out by God Himself, and second, the strategy didn't make sense. God simply told Joshua to have the people march silently around Jericho for six days, and then, on the seventh day, they were told to shout.

However, their first obstacle was the city of Jericho, an unconquerable, walled city. Joshua 6:1

Do you think the walls would have fallen if they said this wall is too big? Or said we will march around three times and shout the fourth time. No, they followed Joshua's instructions. Though it seemed unusual, Joshua followed God's instructions to the letter.

Are we shouting loud enough? There's a time to be silent and a time to shout. What's amazing is when the people did finally shout, the massive walls collapsed instantly, and Israel won an easy victory. God had given the city of Jericho to them before they even began to march around its walls. Joshua 6:2, 16 It was when the people of God, by faith, followed the commands of God that the walls of Jericho fell. Joshua 6:20.

Are you shouting loud enough? The point is, no matter how ridiculous it seems, we must follow God's instructions. The key point is God had already given them the victory before they started marching. Like the Israelites, God has given us the victory!

Prayer

> Lord, give me the boldness to shout for the truth, shout in my praise and worship time, shout when I'm standing up for what's right. Let me shout in advance because the victory has already been won!

Are you shouting loud enough? There's a time to be silent and a time to shout.

WEEK #43

Favor is Not Fair

Exodus 33:17 (ESV)

"And the Lord said to Moses, "This very thing that you have spoken I will do, for you have found favor in my sight, and I know you by name."

God has given all of us an abundance of favor. Have you ever found a front row parking space? Did you say "favor." Have you ever found an unexpected sale item? Favor! I always say, "Favor is not fair."

God is a God that restores what we've lost. Whether it's a job, a spouse, health, or joy. Like He told Moses "I know you by name." Exodus 33:17 (NIV) Reading this made me smile from ear to ear. This is how He feels about us. His gift of favor has our name on it. Sometimes it looks as though we are not progressing. We must remember that our faith is instrumental in recognizing our favor. He's working it out for our good. Romans 8:28

Some people have a misconception that favor is earned. The truth is, we already have God's favor. Our Heavenly Father can turn a situation around that causes your enemies to bless you.

Ephesians 2:8 (NIV) tells us, "For by grace you have been saved through faith, and that not of yourselves; it is the gift of God."

Are you reluctant about sharing a blessing because it might sound boastful? Don't be shy, let others know what God is doing or has done in your life. Give God the glory, this could be a testimony opportunity!

God's unlimited favor is with all of us, and this gift resides in our homes, jobs, health, families, our children and future generations. Exercise your faith by expecting favor today and every day"!

Prayer

> **Lord, give me spiritual eyes that recognize the favor that You have especially for me. Let me appreciate the small blessings. In Jesus' Holy name I pray.**

Reflection

> Our Heavenly Father can turn a situation around that causes your enemies to bless you.

WEEK #44

Stay Charged Up

John 14:16-17 (ESV)

"And I will ask the Father, and he will give you another Helper, to be with you forever, even the Spirit of truth, whom the world cannot receive, because it neither sees him nor knows him. You know him, for he dwells with you and will be in you."

Isn't it a blessing to know that we have an internal compass that we can rely on called the Holy Spirit? We ask Siri, Google, MapQuest and Waze for directions. Are we calling on the Holy Spirit App when we need directions? The Holy Spirit is within us wherever we go to lead and guide us. Downloading is not necessary and updates are never required. Unlike other driving apps that can lead us in the wrong direction, the Holy Spirit will never misguide us.

The Spirit gave instructions to David, and he gave his son Solomon the plans for the temple "that the Spirit had put in his mind."1 Chronicles 28:11(NIV) The Children of Israel ignored the instructions from Moses, the greatest Prophet who was led by the Spirit. An eleven-year journey turned into forty years because of their disobedience.

We can stay charged up by keeping our Holy Spirit apps plugged into the power source of prayer, faith, and God's word. If you go down the wrong road because we didn't listen to the Holy Spirit, make a U-turn, repent, and start over. Continuing down the wrong path can delay the blessings that our Father has planned for us. Stay charged up so that you can hear the voice of the Holy Spirit wherever you go!

Prayer

> Dear Father, let my ears and heart stay tuned to Your voice so that I never get off track. I do I trust that You will lead and guide me in the direction I should go. Guide my decisions, my thoughts and my desires to line up with Your plans for me. Thank you, Jesus!

Unlike other driving apps that can lead us in the wrong direction, the Holy Spirit will never misguide us.

All is Not Lost

WEEK #45

It's Not a Secret!

Psalm 91:1-2 (NKJV)

"He who dwells in the secret place of the Most High shall abide under the shadow of the Almighty. I will say of the LORD, "He is my refuge and my fortress; my God, in Him I will trust."

What really stands out to me in this verse is, in a secret place we are protected by God and can't be found by our enemies. A fortress is a castle or other large strong building, or a well-protected place, which is intended to be difficult for enemies to enter. God is our fortress. When we think of a secret place, it's usually thought of as a physical location. As believers our secret place is in the presence of the Lord. We can also view the secret place as a safe place where we can tell God anything. Moses' encounter with God in the book of Exodus is a good example of the secret place. Psalm 27:5 (NIV) says, "For in the day of trouble He will conceal me in His tabernacle; in the secret place of His tent He will hide me; He will lift me up on a rock." (NASB 1977)

We can find guidance in a secret place. It's where the Holy Spirit dwells. It's an oasis and is a place that we can abide in.

Distractions, discouragements and disappointments will come to obstruct the path to the secret place. Remember, we have to outsmart the enemy because his plan is to keep us from getting to this place of rest. I wish I could tell you that arriving at this place is automatic, we have to sometimes fight to get there. But, when we arrive, it is well worth it! How do we fight? With the word of God. What is required of us to enter God's rest is to follow the directions found in Hebrews 3:1 and Hebrews 12:3. Those scriptures tell us to "consider" Jesus.

When we take our eyes off ourselves and the situations we are facing and focus only on Jesus, the path to the secret place – the place of rest – always becomes crystal clear. When we remind ourselves that it's all about Him – always has been and always will be – the only thing that remains is for us to do is to rest! Don't keep this secret place a secret, let's share it with others.

Prayer

> **My Lord, lead and guide me to Your secret place. Hide me from all of the external and internal noises that try to keep me from dwelling with You my safe haven. In Jesus' Holy name!**

When we take our eyes off ourselves and the situations we are facing and focus only on Jesus, the path to the secret place – the place of rest – always becomes crystal clear.

WEEK #46

We are Anchored

Acts 27:29-31 (ESV)

"And fearing that we might run on the rocks, they let down four anchors from the stern and prayed for day to come. And as the sailors were seeking to escape from the ship and had lowered the ship's boat into the sea under pretense of laying out anchors from the bow, Paul said to the centurion and the soldiers, "Unless these men stay in the ship, you cannot be saved."

Isn't it amazing how a big boat is anchored? When I sailed in the Caribbean Islands, it was unexplainable how a big boat could be anchored into the water and be moved by the wind. I didn't have any doubt that the large vessel would not sink. Do we have more trust in God than we do in a boat not sinking? We should because He is the anchor of our souls. Hebrews 6:19 tells us that "hope anchors the soul." Notice how Paul told the centurions and sailors that they must stay with the ship to be saved.

"Men, I can see that our voyage is going to be disastrous and bring great loss to ship and cargo, and to our own lives also." Acts 27:10 (NIV) Do you think that perhaps the Holy Spirit revealed to Paul that it would be safer to stay in the ship to be saved? Has there been a time when the Holy Spirit revealed something to you that helped you make a good choice? Paul's decision not only saved his life, but it also saved the lives of others.

Paul explains all in Acts 27:23-24 (NIV) Listen to what he said: "Last night an angel of the God to whom I belong and whom I serve stood beside me and said, 'Do not be afraid, Paul. You must stand trial before Caesar; and God has graciously given you the lives of all who sail with you." What a remarkable promise for God to make! In fact, it's the type of promise only our Heavenly Father could make. Only a sovereign God who is stronger than nature can promise to save people from a storm. Only a God who created the wind and the waves can guarantee that they will not take the life of a specific ship's company.

Acts 27:40 (ESV) says, "So they cast off the anchors and left them in the sea, at the same time loosening the ropes that tied the rudders. Then hoisting the foresail to the wind they made for the beach."

God is our anchor, and He keeps us from drifting unnecessarily. Have you ever found yourself drifting away from peace, joy, and hope? I know I have. He is our Anchor who keeps us from drifting. Don't forget that God is waiting to take us back to shore when we drift away, just like He did for Paul and the sailors. Don't forget that we can never drift too far away from God's presence even when the storms of life are raging.

Prayer

> Lord you are my Anchor. Let me hold on to You when I drift away. Lord let me be reminded that You are always available to bring me back to shore when I feel lost, disappointed or need guidance. You are the anchor of my soul! Thank you, Jesus!

Reflection

God is our anchor, and He keeps us from drifting unnecessarily.

WEEK #47

You Are Stronger Than You Think

2 Corinthians 12:10 (TPT)

"So I'm not defeated by my weakness, but delighted! For when I feel my weakness and endure mistreatment — when I'm surrounded with troubles on every side and face persecution because of my love for Christ — I am made yet stronger. For my weakness becomes a portal to God's power."

How can we be strong if we're weak? Doesn't this sound contradictory? Were your greatest achievements accomplished through a feeling of inadequacy? Like Paul, when we admit that we're weak it allows God to take control. It also strengthens our faith.

"But he said to me, "My grace is sufficient for you, for my power is made perfect in weakness." Therefore I will boast all the more gladly about my weaknesses, so that Christ's power may rest on me." 2 Corinthians 12:9 (TPT)

When we realize that all we need is God's Grace we can live our best life ever! The beauty is, grace is not anything that we have to work for, because it's free. I love the old hymn "Amazing Grace", especially the lyrics "how sweet the sound, that saved a wretch like me…" Hallelujah!

"Pride goeth before destruction, and an haughty spirit before a fall." Proverbs 16:18 (KJV)

When we are humble, pride is thrown out the door. Paul walked in humility. Pride can hinder us from receiving all that God has for us. It's a spirit that can creep upon us in a subtle way. Ways like, "I don't need help," "I don't want anyone to know," "I'm fine." How can we become weak within Jesus? We have to identify and admit when we have issues. After all God knows and He's waiting for us to surrender. Most importantly, don't suffer in silence.

When we give our all to Jesus, He gives His all to us. Whatever your all is, surrender to him so that through your weakness, you can be made strong. He's the same God yesterday as He is today. Give Him your all.

"And you will know the truth, and the truth will set you free." John 8:32 (NKJV)

Being honest about our weaknesses may seem like we're a failure, or we might feel embarrassed. However, it shows strength and trust in God. When we are transparent, we also help others. Let's throw away the pride and practice transparency and proudly become weak so that we can become stronger in Christ!

Prayer

> **Lord help us to let our guards down and not be concerned about what someone thinks about us. Let us focus on what Your word says about us. In Jesus' name, Amen!**

Reflection

When we realize that all we need is God's Grace we can live our best life ever! The beauty is, grace is not anything that we have to work for, because it's free.

WEEK #48

Restoration

Psalms 23:2-3 (TPT)

"He offers a resting place for me in his luxurious love. His tracks take me to an oasis of peace, the quiet brook of bliss. That's where he restores and revives my life. He opens before me pathways to God's pleasure and leads me along in his footsteps of righteousness so that I can bring honor to his name."

Restoration is a beautiful thing. Isn't it gratifying to see something old turn into something new? Have you ever observed how old wooden floors are restored? After the top layer is removed, a new unfinished floor is sanded down beneath the surface. This is what we look like when we surrender our lives to God. I had this experience whereby brand-new beautiful hardwood floors were installed incorrectly. I was so alarmed because from looking at the top layer, I thought the floors were damaged. To my surprise after the top layer was sanded down, the floors looked better than the original ones. This is what we look like when we allow God to restore us.

Sometimes we feel like an old floor that has been walked on, scratched, dirty, and beat up from life. But God! He comes in and restores us. How many of us have felt like giving up then suddenly we were restored? You see, our Father can take all our deficiencies and make them new. All we must do is surrender. If He can restore Paul, a man that persecuted the church, He can restore us! Elijah, the man of God, came to this widow's house and brought restoration and recovery to their lives. 1 King 17:15-16.

Wherever people of faith are, there is the restoring of life. Like floors, restoration requires sanding down the first layer which leads to feeling vulnerable because when the first layer is gone, we're bare. The good news is, this is where God works miracles. "Restore to me the joy of Your salvation and grant me a willing spirit, to sustain me." Psalms 51:12 (NIV)

What is your first layer? Is it shopping, anger or doubt? Are you reluctant to let God take off the first layer because you're fearful of what you might look like? However, when we remove that layer, God will restore us, and we will look and feel better. The unfinished surface is where He gives us a new walk, a new talk, joy, peace, and a new life. Let's remember to share this with someone who is feeling defeated, depressed, tired, and just feels like giving up. Take off that top layer, put on joy and peace and experience your deserved freedom!

Prayer

> **Lord give me the courage not to run from you but to You. Let me be transparent and accept how You created me. I will not allow shame, doubt or anger to get in the way of who You called me to be. In Jesus' name!**

Reflection

Sometimes we feel like an old floor that has been walked on, scratched, dirty, and beat up from life. But God! He comes in and restores us.

An Attitude of Gratitude

WEEK #49

Our Attitude Determines our Gratitude

1 Thessalonians 5:18 (NKJV)

"In everything give thanks; for this is the will of God in Christ Jesus for you."

In everything? In a pandemic? Yes! When things are going great? Yes! Give thanks for everything. Why? Because it's the will of God for us. He deserves the glory and honor.

David is a great example of someone who gave thanks. He wrote a number of psalms that were written in horrible situations. He was hiding from his enemies, abandoned, betrayed, thirsty and hungry. Just like David, the Holy Spirit has delivered us from so many unpleasant circumstances. He gives us the strength needed to conquer any battle. Give God credit for everything. He deserves the glory and honor!

"With a freewill offering I will sacrifice to you; I will give thanks to your name, O Lord, for it is good." Psalms 54:6 (ESV)

David thanks God for his goodness, and he doesn't wait until the trouble stops or the worry fades but he gives thanks in the midst of the trial. He practices thanksgiving in the wilderness and doesn't wait until he's safely back at home in a warm room by the fireplace. Let's thank our Father because He is good. He deserves the glory and honor.

"Make a joyful noise unto the LORD, all ye lands. Serve the Lord with gladness: Come before his presence with singing." Psalms 100:1-2 (KJV)

Isn't it amazing how close to God we feel when we praise Him through worship music? It draws us closer to Him. We feel the Lord's presence. David understood the power of giving, thanks to God, through praise and worship. His confidence in God was strengthened because he remembered how many times God delivered him from his enemies. One of David's greatest weapons was his praise and thanksgiving. Listening to worship music will remind us of His goodness. When you're feeling discouraged, listen to worship music. When you're feeling great, listen to worship music. He deserves the glory and honor.

"Give thanks to the LORD, for he is good; his love endures forever." Psalms 136:1(NIV)

Expressing gratitude signals the brain to respond in a positive way. It promotes joy. Share with others how good God is and what He's done for you. He deserves the glory and honor.

"I bow down toward your holy temple and give thanks to your name for your steadfast love and your faithfulness, for you have exalted above all things your name and your word. On the day I called, you answered me; my strength of soul increased." Psalm 138:2-3 (ESV)

David is reflecting on how God has delivered him in the past. Celebrating our victories in advance is letting God know that we trust Him based on what He has done before. Our gratitude changes our attitudes. We can't wait until our faith is bubbling over for us to be thankful. Let's practice thanksgiving even in those uncomfortable moments. He deserves the glory and honor! "I will give thanks to you, LORD, with all my heart; I will tell of all your wonderful deeds." Psalms 9:1(NIV)

Prayer:

> Mighty God, we thank You for the good and bad times because we are confident that You have our best interest at heart. Let us continue to give You the glory, praise and honor because You are good, and You deserve it. Let us rejoice in the wilderness knowing that when we come out, we will see victory. It is only through Your strength that we can do this. We thank You in advance for all of the good things You have planned for us. We give You all of the honor and glory in Jesus' mighty name we pray!

Reflection

Expressing gratitude signals the brain to respond in a positive way. It promotes joy.

WEEK #50

Small Things Still Matter

Colossians 3:2 NKJV

"Set your mind on things above, not on things on the earth."

Have you noticed how small things that once made people happy are no longer important? What ever happened to dreaming about owning a home with a white picket fence and having a dog named Spot? Or, reflect on your dream? What Christ has given us outweighs anything that man can create.

"For what profit is it to a man if he gains the whole world, and loses his own soul? Or what will a man give in exchange for his soul?" Matthew 16:26 (NKJV)

The greatest gift is our eternal state or our forever home. Having nice things is great, however, what is most important is our soul. Jesus is the greatest asset that anyone could ever have. Our salvation is more valuable than silver or gold. Let's not forget to share this with others and remember to value the wealth we have.

Here's a quote from Dr. Charles Stanley of "In Touch Ministries", "Recognizing that the Lord is in control of our material wealth helps us with two things: it frees us from discontentment of greed and allows us to be generous, because we never have to fear that we won't have enough.

And my God will supply every need of yours according to his riches in glory in Christ Jesus. Philippians 4:19 (ESV)

Prayer

> I thank you Lord for the small things. Give me a continuous heart of gratitude. In Jesus' name, Amen!

Having nice things is great, however, what is most important is our soul.

WEEK #51

There is a Plan for "Your" Purpose

Jeremiah 29:11 (NIV)

"For I know the plans I have for you," declares the LORD, "plans to prosper you and not to harm you, plans to give you hope and a future."

This is a verse that we've heard often. But today, I want you to read it twice with a personal meaning. Sometimes, our purpose is right in front of us. If you wear glasses, have you ever looked for them and they were on your face? Or, the old saying "if it was a snake, it would have bit me." Some of you already know what your purpose is. Some of us are confused about what God has called us to do. You might be saying, *what is my purpose?* Have you ever entertained the thought that your purpose could be tied to someone else?

The apostle Barnabas' purpose was to encourage Paul. Barnabas guided Paul by spending time with him and letting Paul observe him interact with new believers at Antioch (Acts 11), church leaders (Acts 13), and non-believers in their first missionary journey. Barnabas was comfortable supporting Paul.

Although Paul was called to be an apostle by the will of God, his acceptance into the apostolic community came through sponsorship by Barnabas. (Acts 9:26-30) Barnabas' mentoring relationship played an important factor in Paul's development in becoming an influential leader in the early Christian church. Paul's second journey was without Barnabas. Instead, Silas went with him. Barnabas' next journey was with John Mark. It's possible for us to have a seasonal purpose with different people, which means our purpose can change. Don't be alarmed if your purpose changes. Continue to trust God to direct your path.

Regardless of what season we're in, we all need someone to pour into our lives and mentor us, we all need someone who can labor and work alongside us, and we need someone to whom we can pass on the wisdom and knowledge God has given us. Just because we're not leading a ministry, on the worship team or on the prayer team doesn't mean that God can't use us in a mighty way! Your position doesn't determine your purpose! There's value wherever God places us. Look at David, he was a Shepherd boy in the process of becoming king. Caring for sheep was not a prestigious position, however, David was good at what he did. While keeping sheep, God was preparing David to be the next king over His kingdom. Much of what he learned leading sheep he applied as a leader of men. God wants to know if He can trust us before He promotes us to our purpose and promise. Whatever you do, do it with excellence!

Prayer

> **Dear God, let me live a life that is appreciative of Your plans for me. Let me not forget to remember that my position does not determine my purpose and that You already have everything worked out for me. Thank you, Jesus!**

> God wants to know if He can trust us before He promotes us to our purpose and promise.

WEEK #52

What is Your Story?

The Parable of the Lost Coin. Luke 15:8-10 (TPT)

"Jesus gave them another parable: "There once was a woman who had ten valuable silver coins. When she lost one of them, she swept her entire house, diligently searching every nook and cranny for that one lost coin. When she finally found it, she gathered all her friends and neighbors for a celebration, telling them, "Come and celebrate with me! I had lost my precious silver coin, but now I've found it." That's the way God responds every time one lost sinner repents and turns to him. He says to all his angels, "Let's have a celebration, for the one who was lost, I have found!"

If you asked me for one dollar and I gave you one hundred pennies, how would you respond? Do you value pennies as having less value? Why does it matter? Like the lady with the lost coins, if we look at the currency as souls, pennies are more valuable because we have more lost people to disciple!

This devotional is intended for us to view things like Jesus does. The world validates us on how things appear, God looks at how we love and encourage one another. He took the time to give the believers His perspective in a way that we could understand through parables and storytelling. When we're reaching out to the lost, let's take the time to explain our story in a way that others will understand. Create your parable today.

Prayer

Lord let my stories bless others. Help me to share my stories in a way that glorifies You. Create in me new stories and dreams. In Jesus' name, I pray.

Reflection

The world validates us on how things appear, God looks at how we love and encourage one another.

Tina Hightower-Garrett

Tina is a co-author for the Devotional and Prayer Journal, A Divine Healing Journey. She was born and raised in San Francisco. Tina is a wife, mother of three with an army of grandchildren and great grandchildren, and a Miniature Schnauzer named "Bobby Earl." Tina enjoys spending time with her family and traveling around the globe with her husband. She served as a volunteer as an Assistant Golf Coach for The First Tee of Contra Costa. Her ultimate feeling of joy is encouraging people of all ages.

Tina's passion is writing uplifting devotionals in an illustrative way that connects yesterday with today. Graduating from a School of Ministry gave her a better understanding of the Bible. Tina serves with Grace Living Ministries, a faith based women's ministry that encourages women with their walk with the Lord. After retiring, Tina and her son became business partners. Legacy plays a very important role in her life. "We must teach our children to rise up and use their God given talents." Psalm 78:6 - reminds us that the generation to come might know, even the children yet to be born, that they may arise and tell them to their children.

Wandah Mitchell Parenti

Two-time Amazon Bestselling Author, Wandah Mitchell Parenti, is a co-author for the Devotional and Prayer Journal, A Divine Healing Journey. Wandah was born in the Bay Area, but raised in Southern California. She is a true Native of California. Wandah is a loving wife, who enjoys being a mom, and Mimi. Wandah's passion is coaching and mentoring women which she has

been purposefully fulfilling for years. Upon completing ministerial studies, she began applying her faith and became a volunteer counselor and educator for post-abortive women. Wandah also serves as a faith based Crisis Counselor for National Alliance on Mental Illness.

Connect with Wandah:
www.wandahparenti.com
Instagram - Facebook - Twitter
@wandahparentiauthor

www.ingramcontent.com/pod-product-compliance
Lightning Source LLC
Chambersburg PA
CBHW050726010526
44107CB00009B/755